Praise for *Hidd*

"The first time I ever met Janna was at a conference where she shared a story about a season of walking through grief. What I loved then—and now, about her, was her willingness to wrestle with the hard questions provoked by suffering, and her willingness to fight for faith when all felt lost. The world needs tender-hearts like hers, who aren't afraid to tell their stories, and in doing so, reach out a hand to others, who need to know they aren't alone. Janna is such a soul, and such a writer."

Kris Camealy, Author of *Everything is Yours*, and Founder/Director of Refine {the retreat}

"It is difficult in seasons of suffering and grief to believe in a good God. We need voices like Barber's to challenge a culture of denial with radical honesty and vulnerability."

Helena Sorensen, Author of *The Shiloh Series* and *The Door on Half-Bald Hill*

"Janna Barber is not afraid to sit in the tension and paradox of spiritual transformation. Her words bring a welcome, gentle, and wise voice that help me see my own journey and the journey of others with more tenderness and compassion."

Jill Phillips, Recording Artist and Therapist

"Frederick Buechner said, "Listen to your life." That's exactly what Janna Barber has done in the pages of her new book Hidden In Shadow. Although you may not have grown up a preacher's daughter who later became a pastor's wife, you'll appreciate these honest and vulnerable stories pointing to the truths universal to us all."

John Blase, Poet and Author of *Know When to Hold 'Em: The High Stakes Game of Fatherhood*

"Honest, brave, and timely. Hidden in the Shadow is a beautiful book that reminds us that grief and doubt are holy, and that to hold both the beautiful and the messy in the same hand is to live a fully human life."

Jerusalem Greer, Author of *At Home in this Life*

"These days, so many leaders attempt to move the masses by reducing the world to lists and bullet points. Such reductions may benefit wars, but they are of no real help to lonely pilgrims who need the warmth of a human companion. Janna Barber's writing zooms in instead of zooming out, asking the reader to consider a single life story rather than a vast treatise. With humility and with honesty, she doesn't attempt to dominate, only to begin a conversation. She invites us into the, "This is what I have seen," an approach to dialogue I find both vulnerable and refreshing."

Rebecca Reynolds, Author of *Courage, Dear Heart*

"Memory. Remembering. Through her writing, Janna Barber gives us permission to remember that having faith in the unseen is just as authentic and plausible as believing the moon still exists even when it's hidden from view. Through her prose, Janna Barber courageously lays out her life on the page before us, as if at an altar, saying, 'Here I am, here are my memories; they are sacred, not because they are delightful, but because the pain infused in them has the odd effect of blessing the hearer of memories."

- Eric Peters, Singer-Songwriter and Visual Artist

"There are lots of personal reflections on faith to be found on the virtual bookshelves of the internet. Why choose this one? For one, Janna is a remarkably fluid and coherent writer--an accessible artist. Much more importantly, she's honest. The truth is to be highly prized in our era, especially when it isn't self-absorbed or self-serving. Janna brings her enormous talent to the most difficult of subjects (faith and grief) in a way that will challenge, disturb, and ultimately console our broken hearts."

Thomas McKenzie, Author of *The Anglican Way*

Hidden in Shadow

Tales of Grief, Lamentation, and Faith

Janna Barber

ghost choir

Thistle Bound Press
1008 Timber Ridge Rd.
Bluff City, TN 37618

ghost choir is an imprint of Thistle Bound Press,
www.thistleboundpress.com

Chapter six of this book was originally published in The Molehill, Volume 4 by Rabbit Room Press, 2016, under the title “Cinnamon.” Used by permission.

ISBN-13: 978-0-9979685-2-1

Hidden in Shadow

"JOY AND SORROW ARE THIS OCEAN . . . "

- RICH MULLINS

To Mom and Dad,
All is forgiven–just kidding, all is grace.
I love you both, and am so proud to call you mine.

To Risha and Jonathan,
my companions on this family roller coaster,
this book is for you.

And to John,
Thank you for being the number ONE fan of my writing.
I'll never stop being grateful for your support.

Preface

The moon travels thirteen degrees per day, taking a full month to complete its orbit around earth, all the while shining an ever-changing reflection into the night sky. Except for those few nights in the middle of each rotation, when the moon disappears from sight. After observing this phenomenon for thousands of years, you'd think humanity would have developed more of an ability to believe in things we can't see. Yet it seems for many of us, that the more trips we make around the sun, the less we believe.

Sometimes, when the moon is nice and full, it looks like a golden-orange plate, so close you could eat off it. Other nights you can barely see a sliver way out in the sky, but the glow it provides is still reassuring. Even though it's always changing, we say things like "he was as constant as the moon." But what about those nights with no moon, when the black sky is filled with bright stars, or storm clouds block our view of the moon? On those nights it can be hard to imagine an enormous yellow rock floating out there in space, let alone that it will soon reappear. Yet, despite all our doubting, the cycle of the moon never wavers. It happens over and over, month after month. Waxing and waning, again and again.

I'm afraid my faith cycles through similar phases. When it's strong and healthy, its light pervades every corner of my heart, and I can't picture it any other way. But shadows of darkness and doubt show up pretty often, and little by little, I lose sight of my faith altogether. This cycle repeats itself more often than I'd like, or more often than I'd like to admit, anyway. Yet whether I admit it or not, here on planet earth, change is inevitable.

When I was little, God was as real as the sour green clover that grew along the edge of our yard, his love for me as immediate as the tang I felt on my tongue whenever I popped one of its torn leaves into my mouth. Even though my family moved around a lot, even though we faced struggles and I often felt sad, my belief in God was strong. I knew he was true. I never doubted his power, or his goodness. I believed he died for me, and because of my belief, would one day take me to heaven, to live with him forever. There were no big questions during those early days in the desert. Like Moses after the great Exodus, I had no idea where I was headed, but I didn't need to know. It was enough for me to be going there with my family. I didn't need a map because I trusted the one who led us. I felt his cloud of protection during the day, I'd seen his pillar of fire glowing each night, I remembered the walls of water he created from the Red Sea. The promised land was just ahead; and I would never turn back.

Once, when I was very small, I went to bed early, all by myself; but I couldn't fall asleep. It was around eight o'clock, but still light outside. The windows were cracked, and a warm summer breeze fluttered in through sheer, fluffy curtains. I don't remember what house we were living in at the time, but the entire room feels yellow in my memory, from the paint on the walls to the fabric I was curled beneath. As the sunlight faded, I began to feel scared and alone, so I decided to pray, thinking God could help me feel less afraid. With childlike faith I asked him to hold my hand until I fell asleep. Then I slid my hand out from under the covers and laid it on the pillow beside my face. I unfolded my fist and waited. Just as I began to doze, I felt a light, gentle pressure in the middle of my palm, so I squeezed it back and drifted off to sleep.

Years later, all those days of wandering in the wilderness started to take their toll, and my faith–like the everchanging light of the moon–began to fade.

In my thirty-eight years of following Christ, I've seen my faith cycle through many different phases. Some of them were very bright and some of them have been quite dark. I sometimes hesitate to admit when I'm in a bright phase, for fear it will fade. Those are the times I can see the invisible God in so many visible ways: when the bread is broken in front of me at communion, when I sip the bitter wine, when tears roll down my cheek, unbidden, in response. When I step onto my porch, take a deep breath and look out at the world around me, I see Christ everywhere. How could I not? He seems painfully obvious.

I know he's not obvious to everyone and I don't want to sound like I walk around in a holy bubble. It's just that on a good day, I'm able to feel grateful for my senses. But since that isn't always the case for me, I try to savor that blessing when it occurs.

What a thrill it is to smell smoke from cedar logs, burning several blocks away. To see a rainbow refracting from the light of a misty grey sunset, to stroke the leaves of a crepe myrtle, or pinch the hearty bud until the delicate bloom bursts open. To hear, there is so much to hear: the bells ringing in an old chapel I didn't know was hiding in the woods, across the lake from where I like to walk; the low moan of a train whistle, carried for miles on the back of thick, dense fog; the bellow of a thousand frogs on a damp summer evening, and the all-encompassing silence when it suddenly stops. (How do they all know the precise second to end their song?) And finally, to taste. As warm water pours out from the shower nozzle every morning, the tart chlorine like a holy baptism, willing each new day to begin with grace.

But I know what you're thinking, and yes, it's easy to doubt those senses. After all, any time we find something good in this world, evil is lurking just around the corner. And what if that's the real truth after all? What if it's stronger than the beautiful and the good? Isn't that the scariest part about the darkness? To acknowledge God in those times, is to acknowledge the fact that he's the one who turned out the light. And what kind of goodness is that? What, exactly, is the point of chaos and death in our lives? What kind of picture is God painting anyhow? Is his art strictly limited to impressionism?

Because the dark times can feel rather blurry. Those are the days when it's harder to see small human actions as any sort of blessed ritual. Instead, the showers I take are for other people, so they won't be able to smell me anymore. The words I say and hear are half-hearted. The meals I eat are merely fuel, and the things I touch leave me feeling numb. The darkness makes me forget that *every* sensation is sacred, made holy by the fact that Christ himself created it, declared it good, and felt it first with his own hands.

Wouldn't it be easier if spirituality limited itself to cerebral, mystical visions rather than doling out messy, fleshy miracles right in front of us? Isn't that why we run away from the liturgy of physical sensation, by setting our thermostats to comfortable, and coating the air with chemicals 'til every last atom is neutral and pleasant? Because we can drink clean water whenever we want to, and because there is so much else available to drink in middle class America, we have no idea what it feels like to actually thirst. So, we insulate, and we numb, and we wonder where God is. Why won't he just prove himself to us? Why can't he spell out his grace message in puffy cloud letters for everyone to read?

But what language would he use to write it, and what about the other half of the world that's still asleep? Perhaps it's not so much that God is hiding. Perhaps it's just our human perspective, demanding constant light, while God sees need for darkness.

But what if God's impressionist style were yet another form of his kindness, as opposed to the disciplines of realism and abstraction? Could harsh, fuzzy sensations still remind us of goodness, if only we had the faith to receive them? Like locking eyes with a homeless man, who wants more from me than I can give him, or listening to the mournful song resounding from the hollow of his old, beat-up guitar? When I taste bitter acid at the back of my throat because a friend has dismissed me, or when I smell the burnt bagel my teenage son left in the toaster for too long–are those physical experiences somehow beyond Christ's redemption? Is his salvation only a spiritual concept? How about when I touch my cold nose with my cold fingertips and have to struggle to remember what warmth feels like? What might it look like to give God the benefit of the doubt, even during the dark and blurry times, to let all those unpleasant sensations pull me back to him? To stop avoiding life's sensory buffet, no matter how overwhelming it is. To trade numb survival for ongoing abundance.

God made the moon round, and carved craters in its surface, giving it the slightest impression of facial features to apophenic humans. On eastern continents the eyes and mouth are angled more to the side, causing these shadows to take on a shape that looks somewhat like a rabbit. But can you imagine how alarming it would be to look up and see two enormous and meticulously sculpted eyes looking down on you? Like glancing out your window only to find a stranger staring in at you, you'd gasp at the grotesque and invasive feeling in your stomach. Yet I've wasted countless hours begging God for photographic evidence just like that. Haven't we all made wishes at that particular fountain? Haven't we all searched for clear and visible proof? When the truth is that if God actually showed himself to us, we would melt right there in front of him. Mortal flesh cannot encounter infinite spirit without some sort of fallout. Isn't that what led to the death of the Messiah in the first place, the final end to Jehovah God walking around in human skin?

So, what we're left with on this side of the cross is subtlety, a God who chooses to whisper rather than shout. And the question before us changes to something like this: how do we turn down all the other noise, in our heads and in the world, so we can hear what he's trying to say?

One of the ways I've learned how to listen is through writing. Journaling, the act of stringing together all my random thoughts, often feels like prayer. Writing essays helps me tease out the truths God's been trying to teach me. And creating a concrete poem, out of rough, scattered images gives me a better understanding of who God is, and what he's done.

"Listen to your life," writes Frederick Buechner. "See it for the fathomless mystery that it is." *Even if I never solve it,* I want to ask, but before I can finish my question, I seem to sense an answer: "You are a human being, not a human mystery solver. Your job here is simply to be. Be aware. Be still. Be human. Be loved."

For such a long time, I couldn't see how loved I was, and I still forget it every day. But once I began to write about my life, the fuzziness of God's heart toward me began to take shape. I saw color instead of black and white, vivid pictures instead of smudgy blotches. And the more I write, the more I see. So perhaps the stories in this book were written more for myself than anyone else, but I hope whoever reads them might also be blessed by the telling. May these words shine a light into the dark night, building the faith we all need, to believe in moons that can't always be seen.

Kerri Way

2018

When therapy is over, I get into my car and take the long way home. It's July so the AC is on full blast, but the thoughts in my head are louder than the sound of air pouring through the vents. I drive without any music and let the tears fall more freely than I did in Eric's office.

"I learned to be invisible," I'd told him, staring down at the clumps of cat hair on the old oriental rug. "And to not need anyone."

Lyrics from an old Barbra Streisand song suddenly popped into my head and I started to explain that I must not be interested in being one of those lucky "People," but I'd already mentioned Kenny Rogers that session and decided against it, figuring no one needed to know the vast amount of cheesy lines readily available in my busy brain.

We'd been talking about my reluctance to trust people, to believe the good things they tell me, how I'm always waiting to find out the truth about who they really are. I told Eric I had an indelible memory of myself as a little girl, sitting at a kitchen table loaded with canned goods. A "pounding," that's what the old timey Southerners called it, when everyone welcomed a new minister to church by bringing over a pound of something yummy for his pantry. I could still see the big smile on my little brother's face, and hear the squeals of delight from my older sister, as Mom and Dad worked to find room to store all this new bounty.

"How do you get over it when those same people can't wait for you to leave town a year later," I asked him. "And then it happens again in the next town, and the next town, too many times."

"I'm sorry that happened to you," Eric said, in his best counseling voice, and I forced myself to say, "thank you," because I believed he was sincere. After four months, he's earned my trust, but my showing it still doesn't come naturally.

The red light finally turns green and my thoughts wander to a conversation from the day before: A friend of mine told me about a woman he'd recently made friends with. He described her warmth and authenticity with exuberance, but admitted that the woman seemed closed off and cold when they first met. "Is he talking about me," I wondered for a second, before realizing the impossibleness of the question, since we'd known each other for years. "Bet she reminds him of me," I thought, but was afraid to ask, fearing his honest response.

By the time I get home it's lunchtime, so I take some meat and cheese out of the fridge and call our kids away from their various devices. Sam* is home from college and nearest to the kitchen, since she hasn't found a summer job yet and hangs out on the couch with her laptop most of the day. Ben shows up next, laughing about the latest gag he saw on YouTube. Then there's Laney, my middle child. She's fifteen and spends most of her time alone in her room, drawing. You have to knock on the door to get her to respond since she can't hear anything else through the earbuds she's constantly wearing these days.

I wish I could tell her that I know exactly how she feels, that I remember what it was like to be fifteen, but I know she'd just shrug her shoulders and give me a half frown and half smirk. As if to say, "You don't know anything, Mom, but thanks anyhow for trying."

The prospect of food and routine lifts our spirits enough for conversation and before long we're all smiling and engaged, and life feels good. I'm glad to have these children. I'm glad they like each other enough to argue about their favorite cartoons, that they have a history of watching TV together, and playing games, and going out for ice cream. They're not perfect by any means, but who is, and I like how they each bear strong resemblances to me and their Dad.

Sam loves to argue like John, and she's tall and thin and her smile reminds me of what John used to look back in college. Yet she's moody, like me, and obtuse, and socially awkward. Being on the autism spectrum makes her brain work like no one else's I've ever met, and it's fascinating to watch.

Laney has John's eye color and lips, along with my cheekbones and eyebrows. Her hair is naturally thick and blonde like his, but it's currently dyed magenta so you can't really tell. She loves many things passionately, like John, but is much more cautious with people, like me.

Ben looks more like me than the other two, but his personality is much more like his Dad's. He wants to please other people more than himself, and he's still young enough that he enjoys acting silly.

After lunch I decide to go to the coffee shop and write for a while, because I'm trying to make my one passion a priority these days. And as Eric and John remind me all the time, the kids don't need me like they used to. I can trust them to take care of the pets, clean the house, and even buy groceries or cook dinner a few times a week. This is my time, they keep telling me, and frankly, they're tired of hearing my excuses.

As I drive away, I wonder if our last meeting with Eric could be the beginning of something new. What if confessing this fear of trusting others is a first step? What if the prayers of my friends and family are beginning to pay off? Is there healing in the pages I've yet to write? Is this the way God's going to teach me to need people again, by letting them read my words and identify with my life, though we might have nothing in common at all? Is it finally time, after forty-one years, to stop pretending to be invisible?

Sitting with my mug in front of me, I watch the steam rise and contemplate the inadequacy of language when it comes to capturing spiritual life. How difficult it is to describe eternal happenings to those who exist only in time. I've been taught the words justification, sanctification, and glorification in many Bible studies over the years, and I know that justification is what happened when I was six years old, and glorification is what will happen someday when I finally make it to heaven. I also know that sanctification is where I am now; that it's a process, a state of being that's part saint and part sinner–depending on the kind of day I'm having. Or minute, or hour, or year.

Growing up I sang songs about seeing the light, how I "once was lost, but now am found, was blind but now I see," and I remember having thoughts about salvation that were very concrete. Thoughts like: I'm a sinner ... Jesus came and died to pay for my sins ... all it takes for him to turn my heart "whiter than snow" is a good washing... But as I got older, I began to see how one shower wasn't enough for a heart that insisted on getting dirty every single day. Sure, you could follow the rules and stay inside where it was nice and clean most of the time, but eventually you'd have to go outside for something and the dirt always followed you back in, and soon I began to realize that dirt is what we were made of in the first place.

Sunday was a big day at church as we celebrated the launch of a new church plant where my husband will be the Executive Pastor, serving alongside a Black man named Anthony Burton, who'll be the Teaching Pastor. Bridge Church will meet in an elementary school on the South side of Knoxville, and the plan is for it to be intentionally multi-ethnic and multi-cultural. All the families who are joining us and the Burtons to plant the new church came up on stage and the congregation prayed over us. There are only four more Sundays between now and our first official service, and at least two of those Sundays are reserved for practice runs, so it was one of the last times I would attend Providence–the church that's been my home for the last twelve years.

I got very emotional during the final songs, thinking about how I wouldn't be hearing these same people sing every week anymore. I'm excited about what lies ahead for our family and this new church, and I believe passionately in the mission of racial reconciliation, but I'm also sad to be leaving people who feel like family. It's one of just a few times in my life to be leaving a church in good standing, and maybe the only time in my life that leaving a church hasn't also involved a move to another town or another house.

Since my Dad was a pastor, and the longest amount of time he served at a church was four years, I've left behind lots of churches and homes and towns over the years; and ninety-eight percent of the time, I had no say in the matter. People laugh when I tell them I no longer shudder to hear John call himself a pastor, or when I say I prefer to be known as just "John's wife," instead of "the pastor's wife." But few of them understand the legitimate trauma of my past.

Whether it's something as simple and routine as a tonsillectomy, or something as dramatic and unexpected as a car wreck, there's a thread of pain and sadness running through most of my early memories. Yet I've recently learned that the survival instinct is our worst enemy when it comes to memory banks and the general outlook on life we develop during our formative years. It turns out our brains are not much different from other animal species in the way we're always looking to avoid pain and death, and our minds are hardwired to remember all the things that have hurt us in the past, so we can bypass them in the future. The problem with locking down on the negative, of course, is that you tend to forget about all the positive.

I'm sure my parents could tell you fifty happy memories for every one of my sad ones, but alas, the dark scenes are the only ones saved in my memory bank from the first several years. Like when I hid behind the recliner of our new parsonage in Greenwood, Arkansas, reading a letter that had been returned to me. I'd mailed it to my best friend Karen, whom I'd left behind in West Memphis the year before. I cried as I realized we'd probably never see each other again, especially since her Mom is the one my sister had told me about, the one who shouted at her and my Mother as they left the church building the night Dad was fired. "Y'all should've died in that car wreck, you know," she said, "then maybe we'd ALL be better off now."

No doubt we all have memories of crying alone as children, and there's a good chance the memory of what my sister told me is some sort of confabulation, but that's how the eight year old girl in my subconscious remembers it, and she's not one to be easily dissuaded from her convictions. Plus, the fourth-grade version of myself, along with the sixth and eighth grade versions, could tell you a couple more stories whose endings are just as sad. Like the time I was bullied for a whole year but didn't want to tell my parents because the bully's mom was a single lady who went to our church and it was my responsibility to set a good example of Christian love for this kid. Or the time when I was serving in the baby room during a business meeting, and heard my Dad getting fired through the nursery speakers.

Those kinds of memories leave a mark on your heart, confabulation or not. That's why it's such a big deal for me to take this next step in our lives, to try on the shoes I've previously seen as my Mother's–which were always much too large and fancy to fit my small, regular feet–and I know I'll never be able to walk in them as gracefully as she did. But perhaps with lots of time and practice, I'll find my own way to get around.

My friend Dawn once told me that, "faith is a series of resurrections." She's a poet, so she has a way of saying things that stick with you. We'd been talking about our stories, how we'd both grown up in church, how we'd both been saved and baptized when we were little girls, and how we'd both had experiences as adults that made us feel "born again" all over again. Yet the more I think about this upcoming transition, the more I understand that my own need for resurrection just might be a daily one.

Because faith is much more than a one-time transaction, trading a lifetime of bad behavior for an eternity in glory. And while it is, truly, the best exchange you'll ever get, this "deal" does not originate between equals. It's a bit like Geppetto trying to teach Pinocchio how to eat real food when all he has are wooden lips, hinged jaws, and a hollowed-out log for a digestive system. Only the blue fairy has the magic to transform that pile of sticks and strings into an actual living body. And in my life, only the Holy Spirit can fashion my heart–filled with blood, muscles, and veins–into a heart filled with sacrificial, glorified love. One that can beat forever.

** Out of respect for Sam, it should be noted that the name she now prefers is Samantha, as well as the use of feminine pronouns to describe her. However, because this book is told from the perspective of Sam's mother, masculine pronouns have been used before the date of June 2017, when Sam officially came out as transgender.*

Highway 17

1988

I don't remember the first time my faith failed me. I can't recall some cataclysmic event that made me stumble. I only remember noticing that things had gotten darker, and that happened when I was eleven years old, living in Brinkley, Arkansas.

We'd recently moved there from Greenwood, the town we managed to live in for a whole three and a half years. We moved during Christmas break in 1987. Our family typically moved during the summer, but Dad hadn't been able to find a new job before school started that year. So, in the middle of sixth grade, two months after my first boyfriend broke up with me, we packed up everything we owned, including two dogs and one cat, and drove it all from one side of Arkansas to the other.

Now you might assume that a small town in one part of the state is no different than another small town on the opposite side of that state, but when it comes to a state like Arkansas, assumptions are never a good idea. The northwest side of Arkansas is a mountainous forest region, bordered by dry, arid states like Texas and Oklahoma; and it's like another planet compared to the northeast side of Arkansas–a low, flat, farmland, bordered by the Mississippi River. But it's not just the landscape that changes as you move across the state, the people and their attitudes change as well.

Brinkley, Arkansas, home of fluffy Della Gourmet rice and the farce known as the ivory billed woodpecker, is a paradise for tiny, pesky mosquitoes. It's hot and humid in the summer, wet and muddy in the winter, with just a few weeks' pardon in between for fall and spring. It's not quite Mississippi, but it's definitely the delta and the ever-flat landscape stretching on and on reflects the last century of harsh, bitter relationships between the Black and White families who inhabit the land.

There's no politically correct way to say this, so I won't try. There are no Black people in Greenwood–at least there weren't any when I lived there in the early eighties. In Brinkley however, the Black population outnumbered the White by ten percent. Brinkley was also twice the size of Greenwood back then, so when I moved there, after eleven years of living in predominantly White towns, it suddenly felt like Black people were everywhere.

There were Black families living in our neighborhood, Black girls in my classes at school, Black boys on the football team, and Black men and women working at the stores and restaurants where we shopped and ate. The only place there were no Black people at all was the church we went to, where Dad was serving as Family Life Minister–a title that meant he worked with both the youth group and the Senior Adults at the church. One of the main reasons Dad took the position was because he'd decided to become Southern Baptist now, rather than Independent, Fundamental, or Missionary, which were all the kinds of Baptist he'd been before.

The experience of becoming a minority for the first time shouldn't have to be negative, but I think it always comes with a certain amount of culture shock. Especially when your family doesn't regularly discuss race and equality. Especially when one of your parents grew up in a family brimming with bigotry. Especially when the town has as much racial tension as Brinkley had.

The first house we rented was in town, a rambling two story, with a large columned front porch, a covered driveway large enough for two cars, and a huge pool in the backyard. From the outside it looked alright, but inside the walls and carpet smelled like cat pee. The whole house shook whenever a train crossed the tracks just behind our backyard, and we quickly learned that we were a little too close to the east end of town to remain comfortably White. In fact, it only took one slip, breaking the ice and crashing through the surface of our in-the-ground, frozen-for-winter swimming pool, for Mom to decide that this house was not meant to be our permanent place of residence.

My little brother was about nine at the time, and he'd been throwing the football around in the backyard. He was playing catch with a friend, when one of them missed, and the ball rolled out onto the middle of the ice. Mom came out with a broom in order to rescue it. She managed to scoot the ball close enough so my brother could reach over the edge and grab it, but Mom would have none of that. There was no way she'd risk her baby boy falling into a frozen swimming pool, so she decided to try instead. Unfortunately, Mom was not as flexible and strong as she'd once been so when she tried to stand back up after grabbing the ball, her feet slid out from underneath her and she plunged into an icy bath. I'll never forget the heavy sound of her breath as she tried to catch it in the laundry room, stripping off layers of freezing, sopping wet clothes. She coughed and shivered and sent me up the stairs for dry towels. And I ran just as fast as my skinny little legs would carry me.

Oh shit, I said to myself, *Mom could have actually died.* It might have been the first time I feared for anyone's life, but it was not the first time I cussed. Ever since we'd moved, I'd been hearing other kids cuss at school, and I finally gave it a try myself, when the teacher was out of earshot. In fact, "shit" was the word I'd chosen for my first audible cuss, uttered very carefully, in front of all the right people.

How bad could it be, after all? It only meant poop, and I'd heard Mom say "crap" plenty of times. So why couldn't I say "shit?" Yes, all the Christians we knew thought four-letter words were nearly as bad as drinking alcohol, but all I wanted was to fit in at school, for some of the cool kids to notice me. These were the thoughts running through my head that day when Mrs. Smith walked down the hall to talk with the principal. She left a video playing while she was gone, and my friend Londa pulled out a box of chocolate coated marshmallow bunnies to share with everyone.

Londa was rich and everyone knew it. She lived in one of the oldest houses in town and wore only the latest designer jeans. But Londa wasn't one of those mean rich girls you saw on TV in the eighties; she was actually nice, and funny, and everyone else was nice to her in return. When Londa asked me if I wanted a piece of chocolate, some of the other girls had already tasted it and were expressing their dissatisfaction. It was clear that Londa didn't like the candy either and was just trying to get rid of it, playing one of her usual gags, so I took a piece. When I took a bite the chocolate was good, but the marshmallow filling was soft and gritty and much too sweet. It strung out between my fingers and mouth like warm, melted mozzarella.

Everyone was looking at me, waiting for my assessment, and I didn't hesitate.

"It just tastes like chocolate covered shit," I said with a grin, then added a gagging sound for effect.

Laughter erupted from every corner of the room. Even Shantell and Canice, the quiet black girls who were always good and made better grades than me, smiled at my joke.

"Ooh, girl!" someone yelled from the back of the room, "I didn't know you talked like that!"

And just like that, I was hooked. I loved being thought of as funny. It was way better than being smart. Soon cuss words were a regular part of my vocabulary. Well, I only used hell, shit and damn. I was still afraid of the "f" word, and too much of a believer in God's wrath to add his name onto any of my insults. And since I never hung out with the three kids in my grade who went to our church, I got away with it. For a while anyway.

After Mom's fall she and Dad began to look for another rental house, preferably one west of downtown, with no icy swimming pool. I think they were hoping some distance would help buffer the side effects of some of our new friends, mine in particular. Mom and Dad had noticed a not-so-subtle change in my attitude since we moved to Brinkley, and they began to wonder whose influence was causing it. Was it those disrespectful, giggly girls, the ones with made-up eyes and grownup hairstyles, who showed up at our house for impromptu, after school "club" meetings? Were they the ones who prompted me to start shaving my legs without asking Mom first? Were their friendships to blame for my newfound apathy and sassy mouth?

But moving across town didn't help, because it wasn't my new friends who made me want to rebel, it was me. I didn't like how life had turned out in the last six months. Acting out was the only way to deal with it. I was angry because we'd had to move (again!), but I was especially angry about moving in the middle of the year, before I could even finish elementary school. I was angry we'd moved to a place so different from any place I'd known before, and how this new place made me feel ugly, and poor, and alone. But mostly I was angry that every time I felt vulnerable enough to say I didn't like it there; Mom and Dad would lecture me with biblical anecdotes and pious cop-outs.

"Paul and Silas went to *jail*, honey," my Dad would say, his voice sounding the way it did coming from the pulpit, "and *they* still thanked God." He looked down at me, "They even sang songs, Janna" he continued, "while they were still stuck in *prison*."

"The church your Dad works for is here, Janna," Mom would say, "not there." As if it had always been that way. As if living in Brinkley were no different than living in Greenwood. As if there had been no forced resignation, no six months of unemployment, no tumultuous upheaval from the first hometown my brother and sister and I had ever known.

Not once did they wrap their arms around me and say they understood how I felt. Not once did they say, "we miss our old friends, too." Not once did they say, "I'm sorry, honey. I know how hard this must be on you."

So, a simple change in geographical location couldn't soothe my vicious anger. Mom and Dad could try and shelter me from the world as much as they wanted, but they couldn't stop my adolescence.

Figuring out who you are and what you believe are not easy tasks, and there were many missteps on my road to maturity. The first one happened in school. And while it didn't change my home life all that much, it had a lasting impact on my social one. What's funny is that I thought I'd gotten away with it. I mean, I'd done the worst possible thing–I flipped off my Social Studies teacher–then I managed to convince her I didn't know the meaning behind my gesture. So instead of a trip to the principal's office, and a note sent home to parents, I only had to stand in the corner for the rest of the period.

What had my teacher done to deserve such an attitude? Probably nothing. Ms. Vance was known to have a temper herself, and I was so angry back then that I thought I *really* hated her. Even though she was justified in giving extra homework when we forgot ours, or taking away lunch privileges when we acted up, my friends and I made fun of her extra big nose and extra full lips. She spoke with a nasal voice and pronounced things the way the rest of the black people in town did, which was noticeably different from the speech of me and my white friends, so we made fun of that, too, mimicking her voice and mocking her favorite sayings.

One day she told me to move to the front row because I was making too much noise in the back of the room. It shouldn't have set me off; I'm sure she was right to punish me, but like I said, I was angry—and I loved making my friends laugh. So, I flipped her the bird with both my middle fingers, half-hidden by my notebook, as I scooped it up from my desk. I was looking at my friends, hoping they would see me, instead of Ms. Vance. But Ms. Vance did see, and it made her pretty mad. I'd never been afraid of a schoolteacher before, but I sure was that day. Perhaps it was my fear that made my lame explanation about not knowing what I'd done seem plausible to Ms. Vance. That or she saw right through me and had mercy on me anyway. I'll never know.

Like I said as soon as class was over, I thought I'd gotten away with it. If the principal hadn't been notified, then my parents wouldn't be either. It was in early spring when I committed the crime, but my real punishment didn't come 'til later that summer, when one of the boys who went to church with me decided I needed it.

His name was Jared and he was in my Social Studies class, so he saw everything that happened that day. I never talked to him much, at church or school, but my little brother thought he was funny, and they sometimes played together. One day a few months later, Jared told my little brother the story of what I'd done. Jonathan came straight home and delivered the news to Mom and Dad. I expected a spanking, but Dad knew a better way to get to me. He grounded me, from going anywhere cool or doing anything fun, for two whole months. And on top of that, he made me memorize scripture- various verses about the foolishness of losing your temper, the value of controlling your tongue, and the importance of being a faithful witness. I don't remember all the texts he assigned, but it felt like he'd assigned me an entire book of the Bible to memorize, something the size of Proverbs.

Highway 17, 1988

We'd already moved out to the country when my sentence came, so time with friends became even more scarce than it had been. And the way I coped with it was by retreating more and more inside my head. My "bad" friends had made me mix tapes of the music I wasn't allowed to listen to on the radio. I kept them in an old shoebox under my bed, right next to a folder filled with pages torn from their *Bop* magazines–pictures of the singers and television actors we all had crushes on.

"No, you cannot tape a picture of Kirk Cameron to your wall," Dad told me when I said all my friends decorated their rooms this way. "You might as well set up a mini statue of Baal in your window," he went on, determined to prevent me from breaking the third commandment. So, I started keeping more secrets and hiding my love of the outside world from my parents. I filled up notebooks with lyrics to forbidden songs. I took to putting on my headphones and walking through the rice fields, imagining romantic dates with August Rusher–the red headed boy at my school who all the girls were in love with. I would pretend I was on my way to meet him under a shady tree beside the pond on the other side of the highway, for a picnic lunch. I could see him sauntering slowly towards me, with a red and white checkered blanket tossed over his strong left shoulder. Across his right forearm was a brown woven basket, filled with sandwiches, chips, and two cans of Dr. Pepper.

"You look really pretty today," August would say when he saw me. Then he'd brush back my windblown hair and lean down to kiss my waiting lips.

My imagination became my greatest solace, and by the time I turned twelve, I was an expert at both ignoring pain, as well as escaping into my own little worlds where pain no longer existed. Worlds where my heart wasn't broken anymore, worlds where all the wishes and hopes I'd ever had finally came true. Hidden habits like that, take a lifetime to unlearn.

Soon after my social death came two challenges that shaped my soul much more than forced reclusiveness. The first crept up on the wind, sneaking over rice fields and slowly sitting itself beside me; the second tore through our front door, lambasting, powerful, and defiant. Both challenges happened in the same year, separated by three small months.

Our house in the country wasn't much, just a single-story rental: three beds, two baths and a whole lot of yard placed midway down the road separating the largest stretch of rice fields in two counties. We lived about five miles from town, but the winding road and slow speed limit made for a fifteen-minute drive home from church every Sunday morning, Sunday evening and Wednesday night. Black and orange are the colors I see whenever I think of that house. Like some Halloween poster with thick black trees and bright orange skies, I see us pulling up to the long driveway just as the sun sets, road weary and ready for bed.

It was late June or early July when I knew the world had finally come to an end. Literally. It was nearly dusk, and I was just returning from another long walk, out in the fields behind our house.

But when I came inside, no one was home. There was still one car in the driveway, just like when I'd started out. The other one was out with Dad, who'd gone to visit someone from church, or to deliver one of my siblings somewhere fun. I expected to find Mom in the kitchen or laundry room, but after a few minutes of searching, I realized she wasn't in the house. I walked outside and made my way around the house several times, but I still couldn't find her. Then I began to notice how quiet everything was.

You have to take into account that these were the days leading up to the year 2,000, when all Baptists were sure the world was ending, "soon and very soon." I heard messages about the rapture and the end times at least once a month, and in youth group we'd watch movies about it. Movies whose soundtracks invariably featured the endless beep of a never turned off alarm clock. Suddenly, I was sure of it. I had been *left behind.* I ran around the house two more times calling out for Mom before I sat down on the porch and let it all sink in. Then I started crying and praying and confessing every single one of my sins.

A couple of eternal minutes later, Mom walked up and sat down beside me. Shocked out of my skin to see her, I reached up to hug her neck and my tears regained momentum. After several normal length minutes, I calmed down enough to tell her what had happened. I must have been too scared to feel embarrassed, and too grateful to try and hold anything back.

Mom never laughed at me, but she didn't do much consoling either. You see Mom had great faith in the Second Coming of Christ, and her number one goal in life was to make sure her family and friends would all be ready when the time came for Jesus to split the sky wide open. So naturally she asked me why I was so afraid of the rapture. Did I not believe that when Jesus came for the church, he would also take me along with him? Was there some reason I expected to have to live through the final days of Judgment? Did I think my life truly looked like someone who was living for the Lord? I knew what she was getting at, and I started to think she was right. If I really was a Christian, then I needed to act more like it. So, I repented of my recently acquired sinful habits and determined that when school started in the fall, my friends would see a difference in me.

The first change I made was with my mouth. I'd become fluent in the language of my friends, but I realized it was time to cut out all the cussing. I began by setting small goals for myself. First, I tried to go half a day without saying any bad words. Then I aimed for a whole day. After that it was two; then finally I made it an entire week. Before long, I'd regained my former status of a goody-two-shoes and all was right with the world.

Still, my newly turned leaf didn't seem to have much effect on the rest of the family, and in the middle of October, I began to wonder if my reformation hadn't come just a few months too late. Why else were we being punished again, and who else could I blame but God?

It was late on a Saturday afternoon, and Dad was out hunting with Papaw and some of his buddies in the woods. Mamaw was at the house visiting with Mom and she'd just started frying fish for dinner. The oil was boiling in a pot on the stove, when my little brother came sliding into the kitchen in sock covered feet. He'd had a little cold that week and Mom had been after him to keep his nose clean, so he was running to find her and show her his latest Kleenex to prove he'd done a good job. As he rounded the corner behind the bar, his left shoulder caught the handle of the pot, filled with boiling oil. He tried to jump back, but the pot clattered off the stove and burning oil splashed across his shoulders and face. It's hard to remember what happened next with four women and a young boy in complete panic. I think Mamaw reached for the butter on the counter, but Mom yelled "No!" then hollered for Risha to grab a pillowcase and fill it up with ice. Nothing brought relief to my screaming, scalded brother, and the last thing I saw before taking off for the neighbor's was Mom holding him up in front of the air conditioning vents in her car, turned on full blast.

911 had recently been introduced in the US, but it hadn't made it to the more rural areas of the country yet. We tried to call but when we got a

busy signal Mamaw had the idea to go and fetch a neighbor. I volunteered. I needed to DO something; I couldn't bear what I was hearing so I took off running in the direction of the nearest neighbor's house, half a mile away. I was running barefoot and the sharp, hot asphalt hurt my feet, but I shut it out of my mind knowing it was nothing compared to the suffering of my little brother.

When the neighbor came to the door, I blurted out what happened and she ran to get her car keys, then we both hopped in the car and drove back to our house. Mom was too overwrought to drive, so the neighbor took her and my brother to the hospital, while Mamaw stayed with us girls, making phone call after phone call trying to find my Daddy. Eventually, another neighbor left on his four-wheeler to go search for them in the deer woods.

I don't remember what happened when everyone finally came home later that night. I don't remember hearing good news or feeling relieved, even though I know that must have happened. What I remember most is the huge wall of waiting beforehand. I figured my brother was not likely to die from that accident, but I didn't know for sure, and I couldn't imagine any sort of hopeful outcome. All my brain could manage to do was relive those twenty minutes of insanity, over and over, wishing every single time to find some way to stop it from happening.

In the end the scarring was minimal and there was no permanent tissue damage, but I couldn't help wondering what it meant to live in a world where such scary things happened. Where boys needed to fear running in sock feet, and the girls who loved them couldn't take away their pain.

A few weeks later it was Halloween, and our church hosted a Fall Festival for all the little kids to celebrate. My brother wore a bathrobe over his bandages, and Mom made him whiskers and a crown from construction paper. Then she pinned a fake lion's tail to the back of his robe so he could be King Richard from the animated version Robin Hood. It was a one of a kind costume we never forgot.

I didn't make any new promises to God after Jonathan's accident, nor did I redouble my efforts to invite friends to church or stop listening to rock music. In fact, I can't think of any specific way my heart changed that day. I just know that it did. And not necessarily for the better.

The rest of our time in Brinkley passed quickly. In November I went out for the basketball team, where I learned that talking to Black girls wasn't that different from talking to White ones. I still remember shy, bookish, Canice, who laughed just as much as I did, once she got around her own group of friends; as well as confident, athletic Shantell, whose prowess on the basketball court was something I admired and longed to find for myself. Playing a sport and having a common goal made many of the barriers between us disappear, but my White friends still told the same old jokes and said mean things about Black people, and I was not brave enough to stand up for my new friends.

One day in the Spring, a fight broke out on school grounds and ended in a shooting a few houses away from campus. School was let out early and we were all taken to the gym to wait for our parents. Rumors began to fly about who was involved in the fight and/or the shooting. Most kids figured it was racially motivated. There was a short boy in my class who ran around the gym yelling that his big brother was gonna "whoop some Black ass."

It was scary to think the whole town might be on the verge of a race riot, but things died down in a few days though, and life went back to normal for most of us. The only difference was that the people who were racist before the incident had even more fuel to add to their hatred fire. Many of the towns I've lived in since then have had their fair share of inequality and inherited ignorances, but I've yet to inhabit another city where the tension was so palpable.

I might not think twice about leaving a town like Brinkley these days, especially if I'd only lived there for 18 months. But I didn't feel that way at the end of seventh grade when Dad told us he'd accepted a new job as Senior Pastor at a church in the suburbs of North Little Rock. Moving again was the worst possible future I could imagine. We'd only been in Brinkley a year and a half, and while I didn't love the town, I'd finally managed to make a few friends. Friends I trusted more than our shaky little family. Friends I felt like I'd never find again, and in some ways never have. Those were the days of banding together over something deeper than a common interest; we'd found each other because of our common fears, and a desperate need to belong. Familiarity had just settled into my life again; it was nowhere close to breeding contempt. All I ever wanted in my up and down adolescent life was to wake up and know what to expect. All I ever got was more and more change.

Looking back on our time in Brinkley, it's clear to me now: here's where I learned the art of stuffing. All the anger, fear, and sadness I felt, I didn't know who to trust with it, so I learned to pack it away inside my heart—a lifeboat made of emotion that I hoped would keep me afloat, in a never ending current of change. I've heard people say that depression is anger turned inward, but I think it can happen with lots of different emotions. The more we practice holding back, the more we know how to hold back. So, we keep on practicing. On and on we go, until the inside of us is nothing but a raft of pent up emotion, bound to deflate in the middle of a storm.

Silver Creek Drive

1989

The summer after eighth grade, I was helping out in the church nursery one Wednesday night, when an argument broke out in the sanctuary. We usually had prayer time or a short devotional before business meetings began—maybe that's why the intercom speakers were still on—and when the fighting began I moved closer to the brown box so I could hear more of what was going on. I don't remember who said what or why the whole ruckus started, but I've heard stories since that fill in some of the details. Like how my Dad had started ministering to a homeless man who'd shown up at the church one weekend. How some of the members worried that this man might have AIDS, or they didn't like the fact that he was black. I've asked Mom and Dad about what really happened a few different times over the years, but it's not something either of them enjoys talking about and I don't know if they could even explain it all anyhow. Mob mentality is a real thing, and it happens on Wednesday nights in small Baptist churches. Ask anyone who's ever been a member of one.

Next thing I knew, as I listened in on the meeting, my Dad was standing at the microphone on stage, telling everyone he'd decided to step down from his position as senior pastor. There was no warning, no preamble, just one short statement that changed the trajectory of our family life in an instant. I sometimes wonder if that's really how I heard the news or if I made up an alternate memory to shield myself somehow. My sister says she remembers being in the sanctuary herself that night, how she stood up and told everyone to go to hell at one point, before stomping out the back door. The thing I remember most is standing out in the parking lot that night in shock. All the people who were angry with Dad had driven away and there were a few families who still supported him standing around trying to hold back tears. An older man whose daughter was one of my best friends came over to hug me and I'll never forget how genuine he was. "It's alright now, honey," he said, patting my shoulder as I cried into his stomach. "They ain't worth all this fuss anyhow."

Our worldview was very simple back then, and the only way to explain how some people treated us was to assume they weren't Christians. I wasn't the only one who thought this way. Mom and Dad and all the friends who stood behind them said the same thing. When we were in college my sister came up with a theory that Dad's main job in ministry was to be a last chance preacher, before God closed the doors of a church forever. It would be great if I could go visit each of those churches today to find out if it's true, but I'm afraid it wouldn't be that simple.

Now that I'm an adult church member myself, I know there are many sides to the same story, and you can't reduce complex people and histories to one-dimensional decisions. Getting a group of people to agree on the best way to lead an organization is always tricky, but throw religion, family, and tradition into the mix and things get even hairier. Unfortunately, those are some of the key elements in a small church, where everyone knows who started the church, as well as what family gives the most money to it a hundred years later. Baptists pride themselves on having congregational leadership, and many members—not just elders—can tell you what the bylaws say. In fact, nowadays you can print out your own copy from the church website. They're not the same in every denomination, but the one thing they have in common is their ability to tear a church apart.

Whoever decided church should be run like a business anyhow? Yes, decisions must be made, resources should be used wisely, and somebody has to steer the ship, but why should it be the entire crew? And how much room can there even be behind one wheel? Perhaps those questions make me sound Imperialistic, or Republican, or even Catholic, but I don't care. I'd rather eat pork belly for the rest of my life than sit in a room full of Baptists voting on where to hang up the new coat rack.

In Winter Haven, West Memphis, and Greenwood I was sheltered from the discussions that led to my father's resignations. I was told after the fact, when we had a family meeting and mom and dad told us we'd have to get ready to move again. Those meetings weren't fun by any stretch of the imagination, but at least they happened in my own home, with mom and dad sitting nearby, answering whatever questions they could, giving us the opportunity to express disappointment or offer reassurance that whatever came next our family would be okay.

When it happened in Sherwood, at Indianhead Lake Baptist Church, there was no shelter to be had, only fallout. And when I think back on that night, when I picture the girl in the parking lot wearing sensible shoes and a ponytail, I want to run into the scene and scoop her up and take her out of there. I want to drive her far, far away and tell her she never has to go back there again. I want to shield her from the sad cloud hanging over her house for the rest of that year. I want to tell her that her life is more than this one scene in a parking lot after church. "There's so much more to your life than this moment," I'd say. "No matter how badly you feel right now, things will eventually get better. I promise."

When I first sat down to write this chapter, I was surprised at how much anger came out. How can I still be angry about things that happened almost thirty years ago, I wondered, but then I realized it was because I'd never really gotten angry about it before. Yes, I had sarcastic comments at the ready or passive aggressive hints about the pain that was still there, but I'd never allowed myself to feel everything I needed to feel in order to heal from this particular loss. Initially, there was shock, and eventually there was lots of sadness, but most of the confusion and pain I felt at that time had to be ignored in order to keep moving forward. Life had to go on, so I went to spend a few weeks with my cousins in Colorado, and when I got back, mom and dad had already started going to another church. We barely talked about the place we'd left behind. We didn't know how to. We didn't have answers for all our tough questions, and there were no people in our lives who knew how to walk us through that time of grief.

At this point in my life I can't bring myself to be disparaging toward my parents for not getting us into family counseling or some other sort of recovery effort; I just don't have it in me. I've got teenagers of my own now and I know how hard it is to be responsible for their emotions when I can't even handle my own. So, I won't rail about what Mom and Dad did or didn't do. I'm not angry with them anymore. In fact, I'm not sure who I'm angry with. I barely remember the people who were part of that church, so it can't be them, can it? The fourth and fifth pages of this chapter make it sound like I'm angry with Baptists, or small towns, or maybe just business meetings, but those are nebulous entities I don't know how to approach. Is there anyone I can direct my anger and sadness toward now? And if not, how do I work through all these feelings and get to a place of acceptance and healing?

Great question, but I'm not sure I have an answer for it today. I just know that real redemption can take a long time, and it's not something I get to control all by myself.

I can't fully explain why Dad's lost so many jobs over the years. It'd be nice if I could write a book with eyewitness accounts and first-person descriptions for every church and every disagreement, but I no longer have access to everyone involved, and I was too young to remember all the details myself. And what kind of book would that be anyway? This isn't the Jerry Springer show, and I'm not that kind of writer either. I've often wondered if it would be any easier if Dad had been an adulterer, or a thief, or just a giant jackass. Maybe, but I know a few preachers' kids whose dads turned out to be those exact stereotypes, and I think they'd gladly trade histories with me.

I'm old enough to realize my Dad's not perfect, but I'm also objective enough to see that he didn't deserve to be dismissed the way he was that night in Sherwood. And both the 13-year-old me, as well as the 42-year-old me, long to right that wrong.

"It's all important. It all matters. And it's all being redeemed." That's what I wrote on the whiteboard when I got home from seeing the movie *Eighth Grade.* Our whiteboard hangs in the small hallway between our kitchen and dining room, it's where I put all the things that I need to keep track of. Things like grocery lists, school notes, and other random reminders for various family members, like "clean out the litter box," or "pay the electric bill." I went to see the movie just before we launched Bridge Church—the church plant where my husband serves as Executive Pastor—but I still can't seem to remember what I wrote. When things go wrong, my most common response is despair, not hope. Now, as a Christian, I know I'm supposed to be joyful in all things, but my feelings usually tell a different story. Which makes me wonder if I ever really believed in redemption in the first place.

Eighth Grade is a movie about a young girl's last week of middle school, and I went to see it because I'd been trying to write this chapter, about a similar time in my own life. But as I watched the movie, I found myself relating more to the single dad than his eighth-grade daughter. I guess that makes sense, seeing as how I'm in the parental role right now, with two kids who've already gone through the eighth grade, and one more who'll be there soon. But also, the girl in the movie seemed incredibly selfish and spoiled—completely oblivious to all her dad tried to do for her. The dad in the movie wasn't perfect by any means, but I saw him as a hero for being able to see beyond the temporary circumstances of his teenage daughter's life, and love her simply because she was his daughter—no matter how awfully she treated him.

To be fair, the girl in the movie was forced to endure a *lot* of embarrassing moments; but the thing I was reminded of is how being that age makes you feel like everything is huge. The good moments, the bad ones, the little inconveniences and the major dramas—they're all enormous and unbearable because you don't know who you can trust with your big new feelings. Because part of the process of growing up is learning who to trust. When you're young and innocent, you think the whole world is nice and friendly; but middle school teaches you differently, and if you don't have a reliable adult in your life when the other kids turn on you, it can be terribly lonely.

The girl in this movie has her dad, but she doesn't always come to him because she's afraid he'll turn out to be as awful as some of the kids she knows. The climactic scene happens when the girl comes home after being taken advantage of by a new friend, and her dad follows her up to her room to find her crying beside her bed. Then he gets down on the floor with her and holds her while she cries. There's no sound in the scene other than music, so you can't tell whether or not she told him what happened, but it doesn't seem to matter because later she goes to him for help when she needs to grieve again, and you can see she's learned to trust him after all.

When the movie was over, I sat in my parked car out in the theatre lot and cried. I grieved for the girl and her humiliation. I grieved for myself and the embarrassment of my own growing up, and I grieved over my late start in learning to trust others with my heart and my hurts. I wondered whose fault it is that I can't remember crying on the shoulders of either of my parents when I was a teenager. Is it mine for not telling them I was hurting, or is it theirs for being so caught up in their own lives that they didn't have anything left to give me? Does it even matter whose fault it is anyhow? Aren't we all broken in one way or another, and isn't that worth reflecting on now and again, in order to become more whole?

When I went to meet with my therapist the week after I saw *Eighth Grade* I told him about the scene where the Dad helps his daughter grieve, how much it moved me to see him step into her world and sit there with her and all her big feelings, even though he didn't know what they all were, or even what she was so sad about. Eric's advice to me was to try and be like that father for my children. He said I should experiment with playing that role the next time one of my kids was deeply upset or even super excited, that I should let myself be just as passionate as they are and that might be one way I could affirm the child inside me for whatever feelings she's not been able to express before.

A couple days later I had the perfect opportunity. My daughter overslept and ended up being five minutes late for play practice at her high school. Two minutes after I dropped her off, she texted me to say that the teacher in charge was sending her home. I turned around and drove back to the school to find her standing alone on the sidewalk beside the building. As soon as she opened the car door she began crying, so I hugged her and told her what an idiot her teacher was. I even offered to go in and give her a piece of my mind, which would have been way out of character for me, but thankfully my daughter just wanted to go home.

I wish I could say all my anger was magically gone in that instant, but I'm afraid that would be stretching the truth a bit. I can say that it felt good to agree with my daughter, to not give her a hard time, even though she was the one who'd overslept that day. So much of the time it feels like our responsibility is to teach kids the "right" way to respond, or how to have a good attitude no matter what's going on, but what if sometimes they already know the right things to do and they just need the freedom to feel their own feelings without any judgement? After all, you don't apologize for laughing when someone tickles you, so why should you feel shame over crying when someone hurts your feelings?

Songwriter Sara Groves sings that "redemption comes in strange places, small spaces / calling out the best of who we are." I reckon it still takes the best of me to choose hope over despair these days, so I guess it's alright to leave that note on the whiteboard a little bit longer. And perhaps God will keep working behind the scenes until my redemption is complete. Lord, haste the day.

Julianne Street

1990

When I was little, my favorite place to be was curled up on Daddy's lap. On Sunday afternoons he'd sit in his velvet blue recliner to watch football for a few hours, and I often climbed up to sit with him just before he fell asleep. I'd listen to his slow breathing for several minutes, before drifting off to sleep myself. In those days we went to church twice on Sundays, so the afternoons in between were like a lazy pond in the middle of a cow field–quiet and still, yet surrounded by noise and activity.

When Dad preached, he wore a three-piece suit, with the vest buttoned up, and a coordinating tie tucked neatly behind it. Dad had five or six suits, all in neutral colors like gray, tan, and navy blue. Pinstripes and plaids had gained popularity in men's clothing during the seventies, but Dad's suits were all solid, with conservatively cut collars and narrow lapels. Dad is only 5'11" but when he stood behind the pulpit in his suit, carrying a thick black Bible, he looked massive. And I adored him.

Dad taught all three of us kids how to swing a bat, throw a football, and shoot a basketball. He had huge hands that could build or fix nearly anything, but he was gentle when he played with us on the floor in the living room. Whether he pretended to be a tickle monster that we ran from, a mountain we could climb on, or a launchpad for flying into outer space, Daddy always made us laugh.

Dad is usually pretty quiet, but once he gets going on a topic he likes, he can talk for hours. He loves sports, hunting, theology, and music. On Sunday mornings he woke everyone up by putting a tape of Sandy Patti, or Larnelle Harris, in the stereo in the living room, and turning it up full blast. Dad comes from a very musical family, but he never really played any instruments himself, and his singing voice wasn't the best one in his family. Still, on occasion he would sing a solo on a Sunday night, just before, or sometimes right after, he gave his sermon. He loved telling the stories behind the lyrics to his favorite songs, like "The Love of God," "If that isn't Love," "It is Well with My Soul," and anything by Fanny J. Crosby. His scratchy tenor can be a bit nasal at times, but I still love to hear him sing.

When I was six or seven, Dad tried to fix the heating unit in his office at the church, and it exploded in his face by accident. He was blinded for three days and had to wear two round patches over his eyes, covered with a large gauze bandage, in order to keep out all the light and let his eyes heal. He reminded me of the wounded soldier who turned out to be Shirley Temple's father in *The Little Princess.* He walked around the house slowly, feeling his way around with his hands, and I was scared to get close to him until his sight came back and his eyebrows began to look normal again.

By the time we moved to Lepanto I was too big to sit in Dad's lap anymore, but I still liked hanging out with him whenever I could. I also liked walking to church with him on Wednesday and Sunday evenings. We went early, before anyone else came, and I would sit in the dark sanctuary all by myself sometimes, imagining it to be the most sacred spot in the entire world, with an invisible stream of light shining above me that reached all the way up to heaven.

Lepanto is a small town in northeast Arkansas, halfway between Jonesboro and Memphis. It's the kind of town made up of several generations of the same ten families, who keep running the farms and marrying each other and having more babies. The kind of town with only two gas stations, three restaurants, and one grocery store. There was one Methodist church, one Pentecostal church, and three Baptist churches, including the one just outside city limits. Dad was the senior pastor at First Baptist Church, right across the street from the oldest house in town, where the art teacher at the high school lived.

The town is laid out in a square and on the weekends kids would go riding around town for entertainment, which meant they'd spend a couple hours making the five mile drive in one direction, then turn around and drive the other direction for another hour or so, all while listening to their favorite radio stations and talking to whatever guys or girls they're able to pick up along the way. The joke I was told when I first moved there was that if you ever passed yourself driving alone at night, that's when you knew it was time to go home.

East Poinsett County was the last school I attended before graduating from high school. We moved over Christmas break, so I started there in the middle of ninth grade. For the seventh time in my life I was introducing myself to a whole new group of classmates, at a whole new school, in a whole new town. Six previous populations had mispronounced, misspelled, or forgotten my name already, so this time I decided to change it. I'm not sure if it was a conscious decision. I don't really remember how or when I decided to change it. I just know that the first time a girl my age introduced herself to me at church, I told her to call me JB.

JB was a nickname my Papaw had given me, shortening my full name of Janna Beth to two initials, and the rest of our family called me that on occasion; but now I wanted that nickname to become my real name. Perhaps JB sounded like a stronger person than Janna. Maybe she was the kind of girl who couldn't be hurt by other people, who didn't care that she had moved to a new house and a new town, again. The kind of girl who didn't need to be pretty, or vulnerable, or kind. The kind of girl who'd grown ashamed of her real name, as well as the person behind it.

For the next three years JB was all anyone ever called me. I signed it on my homework pages, JB was listed beside my pictures in school yearbooks. Everyone in our small town, including my coaches, teachers, and friends, took it for granted that I'd always had that name. Some boys at school liked to switch the initials around and tease me, calling me, well... you get the idea. Of course, I'd been so sheltered I didn't understand the joke they were making; I just knew by the way they smiled it must have been rude. So, I'd yell at them to stop, then they'd snicker and walk away.

My two oldest kids are currently going by names of their own choosing, rather than the ones their father and I bestowed upon them, and I can't help but wonder if it's some rite of passage I passed down to them. This need to define themselves according to their own terms, rather than what they've been told by their parents, their God, or their community. Maybe everyone goes through it in one way or another, even if they never change their actual name. Perhaps we all have an innate desire to control the perceptions of others, rather than receiving with grace the vision that comes from the eyes of someone outside our own experience.

When we were younger, we called our parents names like *Mommy* and *Daddy*, but as we got older, they became *Mother* and *Father*. Who changed, was it us, or them? And why? Why do my older kids now think of me only in terms of what I can give them, instead of someone they just want to play with? Will they ever think of me as *Momma* again, like they did when they were children? Are adults ever able to trust someone else to do the heavy lifting, while they rest and wait in response?

The night we loaded up the moving truck to leave for Lepanto I ran away from home. I lit out with no plan at all, just ran out the back door after dinner, when no one was looking, so I didn't make it very far. I was hiding out behind a climbing rock at the park in the middle of the neighborhood when I heard Mom calling for me. She'd been driving around awhile looking for me, and it had gotten dark in the meantime. I hid in the shadow of the giant rock and waited, listening as she called my name. "Jaaaannnnaaaa ... Jaaaaannnnaaaaa ... JAAANNNAAA," her voice grew louder and more desperate with each repetition. I stood there debating whether or not to respond when she called out again "Please come home, Janna ... Our family needs you ... I need you." Then, almost as an afterthought, "You've gotta come back. I know you won't believe me, but we've just gone to war." I finally came out for curiosity's sake, not because I was ready to go back home. Where was home anyway? Certainly not the town we were headed to, but I wasn't old enough to stay behind, alone, in the place we were leaving.

Sometime during the next few days of driving, unloading, unpacking boxes, and watching scenes from Iraq on PBS, I guess this need to redefine myself came to the surface, and I became JB.

The act of naming is an act of separation, as it usually happens when a child is born, and he or she becomes a separate entity, no longer dependent on the womb of its mother for survival. And parents celebrate this new, independent life by giving it a name of its own, filled with all the hopes and dreams they have for its future. But somewhere down the line children begin to take hold of their own futures and determine for themselves whether or not the names they've been given are ones they will keep or ones they will throw away. Sometimes they do both.

I let my own name go for a while when we moved to Lepanto, but once I left for college, I took it back again. My senior year I dated a boy who always called me Janna, and I guess I learned to like my name again hearing it come from his mouth. Jason saw me in a way I had been scared to be seen, but secretly longed for. He saw me as pretty, and smart - worthy of a name that means "God is gracious." Dad had picked it out of the genealogy of Christ in Luke seventeen years prior, but it took the adoration of a teenage boy to make me enjoy it again.

Two years later I was dating my soon to be husband, a guy named John. His was one of those common names that everyone liked to tweak in order to differentiate one John from another, so many of his friends called him Barber, Barberjo, or JB. When I told him I'd also had the nickname JB when I was growing up, he smiled and told me that I looked more like a Janna to him. But on occasion, when he's feeling flirtatious or sentimental–like he wants the world to know we have a connection that goes beyond first names–John calls me JB. And I kinda like that, too.

When God first introduces himself to Moses at the burning bush, he gives only five words to describe himself: "I am who I am." But when Christ shows up thousands of years later, he reads a lengthy passage from the scroll of Isaiah, in order to declare his mission here on earth:

> *"The Spirit of the Lord is on Me, because He has anointed Me to preach good news to the poor. He has sent Me to proclaim deliverance to the captives and recovery of sight to the blind, to release the oppressed, to proclaim the year of the Lord's favor."*

Which description of an almighty, eternal being is more accurate? Who can say? And yet we're told in Galatians that we can call this God Daddy–one of the most intimate labels known to humankind. I believe the Lord is all these things, but there are many times when I can only see one side of him, just like people do with me. We're nearsighted creatures, often incapable of stepping back far enough to get the whole picture.

In her book *Traveling Mercies,* Anne Lamott talks about writing prayers on little slips of paper and putting them in a box, as a way of handing requests over to God. I liked the idea and I tried it out for a few years with the really hard requests, like forgiveness for people who'd hurt me or my family. Those kinds of prayers take time to answer, and it made sense to leave them in God's hands while his spirit worked some magic in my heart. But one day I realized I'd been thinking of God as a CEO, sitting behind a giant mahogany desk, with a three-tiered metal basket laden with prayers. Fine for helping me become a more mature Christian I guess, but what about the days when life left me feeling like a child in need of a nap? Whose lap was I supposed to crawl into if God was only a man in a suit, sitting behind a cold hard desk?

I need more than someone who stands in the pulpit and knows all the answers. I need the man who can get hurt while trying to fix things. I need the man who plays on the floor and sings off-key. I need someone to cry out to in the middle of the night, who knows how much it hurts when the children you've named decide they'd rather be someone else. Because life is not limited to sunny Sunday mornings with frilly dresses and bright smiling faces. Life also gives us dull Wednesday afternoons, dark Friday evenings, and stormy early mornings. It's for those times that Jesus came, to show us grace and favor, in addition to fire and holiness. For God is just as complex and multifaceted as we human beings are; after all, he's the one we take after.

Frances Crawford Hall

1996

For the first half of my life, there was "sacred" and there was "secular," and as the old saying goes, "never the twain shall meet." I don't think I ever heard that message from the pulpit, but I know I saw it in the way we lived our lives in the evangelical protestant pockets I grew up in. We believed God was there for church on Sunday, but we spent the rest of the week in the world, a world quite separate from anything holy. Yes, we prayed before our meals. Yes, my preacher Dad led family devotions on Friday nights. Yes, we had Bible verses hanging on our walls, but the world outside our house was dangerous, so we had lots of rules to keep it from getting in. Like listening only to Christian music, and reading mainly Christian books, and watching mostly Christian movies. No one was selling Christian clothes just yet, but we certainly knew the rules of Christian dress and modesty. We were a people set apart after all, forced to be "in the world," yet striving not to be "of" it.

The idea of experiencing God in things that were not labeled "Christian" was foreign to me. Seeing God in the physical world around me, in the daily grit, and the nooks and crannies of life, was something I never considered, until I went away to college. That was the first time I learned about Lent; from a couple of Methodist friends I made my freshman year. Before that I had thought of God as spirit, and everything else as flesh. Yes, God made the earth and I lived on it, but that's where the connection ended. I never saw the natural world as his present or presence to me. Everything I'd learned about spiritual life prior to leaving home was just that, spiritual. My sins were mainly thoughts and words, and the occasional squabble with my siblings. And the solution to that sin was more words. Words about heaven. Words prayed to God. Words of forgiveness written on holy Christian pages. Words and thoughts were my only connection to the spiritual realm.

It might be hard to understand if you didn't grow up in this same atmosphere, but we Baptists feared icons. Icons led to idolatry, the worship of things which were not God. God was something you couldn't see; so, everything we did see was worldly, and not part of God. Therefore, we would not worship anything we could see. Fine, good. What was wrong with this logic? Well, just one thing. Jesus. You see those southern churches I attended during childhood all loved Jesus. We preached Jesus. We prayed and sang to him. We baptized folks in his name, and we were born again because of his death. We knew all about the perfect, sacrificial life he lived, and we loved to tell the world about his love. But we couldn't hang up a picture of him in the sanctuary. We couldn't place a statue of his likeness in the foyer. We would not allow any images of the cross which still bore his body. For he was not flesh anymore–Amen! He was risen - Hallelujah!! Alive, I say, and living in heaven with God the Father–Praise the Lord!!!

You know, heaven–that far off place none of us have ever seen? That's where Jesus was. Yes, his Spirit was present with us, but he was not inside those tiny stale crackers and sweet grape juice we passed around once a quarter. We did not believe in transubstantiation. We would not stand for such heresy. Communion was a symbol, nothing more, kind of like the American flag. We said a pledge to it now and again, but it was not something to wrap yourself up in every night. That's because our real work was saving souls, scrubbing the sin off those souls, and getting those spiritual souls up to heaven. There was no need to worry about redeeming material things or renewing the world around us. People were dying. Souls lasted forever, but not this world. Therefore! The only hope we worldly humans had was for spiritual resurrection. Deny your flesh, concentrate on the spiritual transformation of your holy soul, and hold on! Heaven comes to those who wait.

Heaven came to me halfway through August in 1994, when I left home for college. Like most of my fellow freshmen, I felt like the whole world was in front of me, and the best part was that I got to make all the decisions. Finally. Now I could decide whether to move or whether to stay put. I didn't have to follow mom and dad around anymore. They no longer had a say in how I dressed, where I went, or how I spent my time. The other great thing about college was the ability to reinvent myself. For the first time ever, I was in a place with lots of PKs, and even more MKs (that's missionary kids), at a small Baptist college, so I didn't feel weird for being a preacher's daughter. Actually, it made me feel like a normal person for once, a normal person who could be whoever she wanted to be. The freedom was overwhelming and wonderful, but I still felt like something was missing. Perhaps that something was a man.

Yes, that was it. To be truly happy, I needed to fall in love; so, I set about trying the best way I knew how. I wasn't asked out on many dates, but I managed to develop crushes on several of my classmates, and I made sure to flirt with all of them. There was a whole new crop of men on that campus and I was determined to harvest a husband.

When young ladies start looking for a spouse, they're either looking for someone just like their father, or else they're looking for someone who's the complete opposite of him. Now I love my Dad a lot, but I knew I didn't want to marry anyone like him. For starters, Dad's a lot like me and I was a fan of the "opposites attract" theory. That's what I saw at home anyway. Mom and Dad were complete opposites, but it worked pretty well for them. Mom always said her relationship with Dad was either fire or ice. "When it's cold, it's real cold," she'd say. "But when it's hot, it sure is nice and warm," she'd add with a wink. My parents got married when Dad was twenty and Mom was only nineteen, and I was inspired to do the same. They struggled financially and argued frequently, yet to me and my siblings they always seemed very much in love. We used to talk about it every time we moved. How we kids had to leave behind our best friends, but Mom and Dad still had each other. It never felt fair.

Even though I didn't want to marry anyone with Dad's personality, I wasn't opposed to marrying someone who might go on to do the same job as Dad. So, I spent most of my freshman year pining away over various Biblical Study majors I found cute. What else would you expect from a young minister's wife in training? Thankfully, none of those clean-cut boys latched on to me that year, so when I returned as a sophomore, I was still single. Only three years left to finish my MRS degree. "A ring by Spring," was what OBU promised its female constituents. Too bad they forgot to mention the 3 to 1 ratio of girls to guys on campus.

In late September, a mutual friend introduced me to a skinny little freshman suffering from his first college heartbreak. Kevin was not the kind of guy I ever imagined dating. He wore baggy pants, oversized flannel shirts, and gave off a general vibe of unkemptness. Kevin struggled to keep his extra-large clothes from falling off his small frame, and I heard he'd been the lead singer in a rap/metal band during high school; but he also had a great laugh, a wonderful sense of humor, and a fierce love of poetry. So even though I thought he was too scruffy for boyfriend material, I was still drawn to him. Kevin wore a soft scraggly beard and long wispy hair that made him look like Jesus in a Da Vinci painting, and after he got over the girl who dumped him, he turned out to be a great friend.

There are plenty of men in the world with long hair, but I'd never spent time with one before Kevin. Mostly because there weren't any in the small towns I'd lived in before college. The only long hair you saw on those guys was in the form of a mullet. Otherwise, the rest of the boys had short, close cuts, because anything else was considered girly. But Kevin had cancer in high school and the chemo made his hair fall out for a couple of years, so I guess when it came back, he just couldn't bring himself to cut it anymore. Kevin became like a younger, wiser brother to me. He seemed to know and really love Jesus in a way I hadn't seen before and there was great depth in him that anyone could see but he never would have suspected himself. Struggling with cancer at an early age gave him life experience that the rest of us lacked. He told the greatest stories and made me laugh in a way few other guys could, that is to say, with sincere snickers, and not just flirty giggles. For two semesters, we were the best of friends. We shared many walks, a few heartbreaks, and lots of jokes. I'm indebted to him for introducing me to a rare and higher breed of the opposite sex: those who knew how to talk and when to listen, and who actually practiced both disciplines. (helping me see that there's more to a man than the width of his concordance?)

Before meeting Kevin, I mostly walked across campus by myself. Most of the time I was hurrying back and forth, from my dorm to class, with occasional jaunts to the cafeteria, but I also liked to walk around daydreaming about my future husband. Like a princess in a fairy tale, I believed my prince would come along someday and take me away to a new home, filled with love and stability. All I had to do was wait for him.

Our college campus was located in a small town in the middle of a picturesque valley, and easily lent itself to laziness and speculation. Wide, well-manicured lawns were skirted by a large river, spacious sidewalks, and a couple of well-placed bridges—which made for perfect imaginary balconies. Many a couple, some knowingly and others clueless, reenacted Romeo and Juliet worthy scenes atop those bridges, sans the Victorian outfits and Shakespearean language.

It seemed my classmates were all feeling the pressure to hurry up and meet their future Christian spouses. We only had four years to make it happen! We all knew the statistics, how marriage rates dropped significantly after you reached a certain age. Well, the girls did anyway. We didn't have the luxury of becoming confirmed old bachelors like the boys did.

Walking alone by myself in the evenings, passing couples walking hand in hand, I dreamt of one day falling in love. I felt like it was never going to happen, that I'd be all alone forever; or maybe God was calling me to the foreign mission field. Did he want me to be happy just to be married to him? I had read books by both Elisabeth and Jim Elliot and dared to hope that if God did call me to missions then maybe he'd let me fall in love with a man willing to go with me to Africa, and hopefully we'd both make it out alive.

Another gift I got at college was an introduction to worship music. Kevin and a few of our friends used to go to Praise and Worship on Thursday nights in one of the campus chapels, and the leaders played music from Vineyard Church, Maranatha! and Hillsong. This music was different from the hymns I'd heard growing up. It felt full of emotion and sincerity. The worship I'd known before that time was limited to three short songs and an offertory piano solo, while members sat stiffly in their wooden pews. When we sang about the wondrous love of Jesus, no one had any heart about it. I remember one man who sang with conviction when he was called upon to deliver a solo every few months, but most church members thought of him as an oddball. He was married to a much younger, much prettier lady in town, and everyone said she only married him for his money. But I can still recall the look on his face as he stood behind the pulpit with his eyes closed, as well as the haunting timbre of his rich, melancholy voice.

Whether I was walking by myself or with a friend, music was ringing in my ears. Sometimes it was the songs we'd just finished at P&W, sometimes it was playing in my headphones. I remember feeling hopeful and free, but a lot of the songs made me cry. There were songs about trading your sorrows and I sang along, "Yes, Lord. Yes, Lord. Yes, yes, Lord," but it wasn't quite enough. I thought about the sadness from my past and I looked up at the moon and felt like it was indeed the face of God. I cried to him when my Dad was dismissed again from yet another church. I talked with friends about the things we didn't like about the churches we'd grown up in. There were moments of despair, but I felt sure they were becoming part of my past if only I could find my way to true love. That would solve all my problems; I just knew it. So, I prayed and prayed for the spouse I hoped God was going to send my way soon.

The summer after I met Kevin, I went on a mission trip to Africa and met Sam, the guy who would soon introduce me to my future husband. I had no idea that would happen in a few short months. In fact, I was hoping Sam could be my future husband. After all, he was really cute and had already lived in exotic places like England and Germany. Plus, he talked about serving overseas someday just like his Dad. He seemed to be my perfect match, except for the fact that he was in love with my roommate.

When we got back to school that fall Sam introduced me to his roommate, John. John didn't go on the mission trip with us. He'd spent his summer working the salad bar at Steak and Ale back home in Florida. John was a year behind me in school, but we soon discovered that we had several classes together because he'd recently switched his major from Biblical Studies to English Literature, and I was a Secondary Ed. major, with an emphasis in English. John was also a photographer for the school newspaper, and I worked on the yearbook staff right across the hall; but we'd never even seen each other before, until Sam introduced us.

At the beginning of my junior year, my girlfriends and I hung out with a group of guys that included John. But as the year wore on John and I spent more and more time alone. At first, I thought he was just another buddy like Kevin because, well, I wasn't attracted to him. He was smart and funny and very sweet, but he was not as clean-cut as my previous boyfriends and he didn't talk about ministry, or missions, or fit into the mold my friends and I had made for who was dateable at OBU.

Then one night I walked into the dark room where John was developing photos and he didn't know I was there. Paul Simon was coming through the speakers, which were turned on full blast; and as he stood there waiting for his pictures to dry, John started singing and dancing ... like a fool. Now John doesn't have a great voice and his movements weren't big or fancy, but the smile on his face was infectious. When I left him at the cafeteria later that night, I went through all the items on my mental checklist. The only box he hadn't checked before was chemistry, but that night there was a spark. A couple of months later we started dating and a year after that we got married.

Sometimes your prayers are answered when you stop trying so hard. And a little music usually helps. Yet there I was, twenty-one years old, entering this great love affair called marriage, hoping love would grant me all the happiness I was looking for back when I was a freshman; but it didn't. Sure, it helped me out a lot with the riddle of life, and the mystery of living in a physical world while possessing a spiritual faith. And yes, it turned me from a lovestruck co-ed into an actual writer and a poet, but it didn't solve the equation of life completely.

Because all the sadness and loneliness I'd felt before meeting John was *not* simply the result of growing up in small churches in the Bible belt of America. For all my conservative theological upbringing, no one had explained suffering in a way that impacted me or changed my understanding of it. I thought that if you loved Jesus and obeyed the Bible, you'd have a happy life. That's the way it was supposed to work. Easy lives were what God owed good Christians. Forget all the examples of righteous men and women who were persecuted for their faith. The reason I thought we'd had a hard time when I was growing up was because of the people who didn't really know Jesus but pretended to. But now that I'd found true love, happily ever after would happen, right?

Wrong.

There's no such thing as happily ever after, here on planet earth. There are only happy moments and sad moments. Times filled with peace and times filled with pain. Your heart is either sick and dying, or healthy and alive. This constant orbit of our lives is either bathed in light, or hidden in shadow.

Locust Street

1999

It's a strange thing to go to therapy for the first time, an uncomfortable thing. Like inviting a new friend over for coffee, then greeting her at the door in a swimsuit. Or opening your mouth for the dentist, when you haven't brushed your teeth in two weeks. When I called to set up my first appointment, the counselor told me that she usually met with clients in the back of a portable trailer, which was currently serving as a crisis pregnancy center.

Just great, I thought, that'll make this easier.

I was twenty-two-years old at the time, living in a large apartment on the lower level of what had once been a two story office building. I lived there with my husband, John, and our newborn son, Sam. We chose the apartment because it was cheap, and close to the college where John had just started working on his master's degree.

I'd recently quit working in order to stay home with Sam, and we were home in that tacky apartment a lot. I remember staring at the dark paneling walls of my bedroom and living room for hours on end, wishing I had someone besides a baby to talk to. For a change of scenery, I could walk into the spacious kitchen, whose walls were papered with flowery Laura Ashley patterns, or sit on the floor of the master bedroom and run my fingers back and forth across the fluffy, bright pink carpet. Then there was Sam's room, painted a bright blue to match the curtains I'd picked out when I was pregnant, but with only one small window in the room, "robin's egg" turned out to be less cheery than we'd hoped.

I drove for thirty minutes by myself on a Saturday morning; then I sat in my parked car staring at the empty gravel parking lot for another five minutes before getting out. As I walked up the wooden ramp made for wheelchairs, Gail opened the door and met me on the porch, smiling.

She was a tall, thin woman, with wispy blonde hair that was cut in a short messy style. She wore flowy printed pants with a plain knit top, a crocheted sweater vest, and not much make-up.

"Well, hey there, Janna!" she said, one hand raised to shade her eyes and the other stretched toward me for a handshake. "I'm Gail," she told me, even though we'd already met each other at church once before.

I grabbed her offered hand and gingerly shook it. Then I half smiled and looked at the ground. "Um, it's really nice to meet you."

She pointed the way into the building for me. "My office is down the hall on the right," she said, "just across from the bathroom."

I walked through the musty, half-lit hallway and sat down on the small sofa in her office, scooting a ragged pillow with faded flowers out of its corner, onto the cushioned seat next to me. Gail sat down behind her beat-up secondhand desk for just a second, before remembering that she'd forgotten to turn on the noisemaker in the hall.

"I can go turn that on if you want," she said, half rising, and pointing to the small box on the floor, just outside the office door. I looked at her with a confused expression.

"You know," she waited, "... for privacy?" I hesitated, blinked, and nodded–a universal sign of understanding.

"But since it's just the two of us here today," she said, lowering herself back into her chair, "it's really not necessary."

"Yeah..." I stalled, waiting for her to offer another option. She said nothing.

"Okay." I finally said, noting the open door, another luxury afforded by just the two of us. "It's fine, I guess."

Gail asked me how I was doing, and I mumbled something and stared at the floor. She was quiet for a minute, then spoke, "Well, if you ever think you're pregnant again, I've got access to free pregnancy tests..." She smiled for half a second, until she saw the startled look on my face. It was kind of a funny thing to say to someone who's come to see you to talk about postpartum depression.

My look faded slowly, but Gail was unfazed.

"Free is always good, right?" she probed. "So, you know, just, uh... let me know..."

We sat in silence for two more minutes. I know because I counted the number of times I kicked my crossed leg: one hundred and twenty-two. Then Gail got direct. "Janna, why did you want to come and see me today?" she asked.

I was caught off guard by her abruptness. I sifted through my thoughts for various possible answers. There was frustration, loneliness, sleeplessness, the severe guilt I felt for being an angry mother. Finally, I narrowed it down to one incomplete sentence.

"Because I'm afraid that I'm going crazy," I told her, looking down at the area rug and scuffed-up wooden floor.

"Why would you think that?" she asked, as if she were a teacher helping me solve a word problem in math. I concentrated on not sounding like a dramatic teenager.

"Well," I sighed, "I guess it's because I'm so mad all the time."

"And why are you so mad all the time?" Gail didn't make air quotes as she repeated my words, but her voice changed tone, like vocal italics, and the word "time" hung in the air between us as I recalled the moment I realized just how angry I had become.

It was two in the afternoon. I'd been trying to get Sam down for a nap but the more I patted and bounced and swayed, the more upset he got. I stood in the room beside his crib staring at the bright blue walls, feeling like I was holding a malfunctioning alarm clock in my arms, instead of a baby. And the only way to get the noise to stop was to smash the clock against the wall and break it. So, this is how shaken baby syndrome starts, I thought to myself. That's when I knew I couldn't keep everything all to myself anymore. I needed help, and that meant telling someone the truth.

"I don't know," I sighed, rubbing the knuckles of my closed fists, "maybe because my baby screams at me all the time."

"What do you mean when you say your baby screams at you all the time?" Gail asked, pulling out a yellow legal pad from the top drawer of her desk.

"Well, he wakes up crying because he's hungry," I told her, "and it's like he can't even wait two seconds for me to sit down, pull up my t-shirt and get ready to nurse him. And while I'm working on it, he just gets louder and madder until he's totally freaking out, which makes it even harder for him to latch on."

"Oh yeah," she said, I remember those days." A smile spread across her face, "Does he nurse a lot during the day?"

"Yeah, like every three hours." Gail clicked open the tip of a ballpoint pen that had been lying on her desk.

"And how's he sleeping?"

"He sleeps pretty well, once he actually gets to sleep." I shifted in my seat and grabbed the old pillow beside me, then looked back up at Gail. She nodded for me to go on, so I hugged the pillow and continued.

"I mean he'll sleep for almost six hours most nights. It's just that he won't go to sleep all by himself, and sometimes he flips out and just cries and cries and nothing we do calms him down... until he finally conks out because he's so tired from crying."

I recounted the scene in our apartment the night before, with John and me taking turns making laps around our coffee table, bouncing and patting Sam on the back for hours, until he finally gave in and slept. Gail listened and nodded, making notes on the pad of paper in front of her.

"I was never a high energy person to begin with," I said, "but you probably guessed that already."

"Why would you think that, Janna?"

"I don't know, because people always tell me that I'm too quiet, too laid back..." It was beginning to irritate me that Gail had nothing but questions. "It's just that I've been nursing Sam for five months now, and I can never get a good night's sleep anymore." I loosened my grip on the shaggy pillow. "I mean, I remember looking at all those baby magazines in the doctor's office when I was pregnant, but my life now, it just doesn't look anything like the pictures I saw then."

"What does it look like?"

"It looks like me... sitting on my couch... half naked all the time." I put the pillow down next to me, then picked it up again. "I'm always covered in drool or spit up. I'm always holding a crying baby. Or rocking him, or burping him. Or cleaning up his shi–Sorry. I guess I shouldn't say that word."

"Oh, don't worry about that," Gail quipped. "You can say all the cuss words you want to in here." She smiled before speaking again. "So long as you don't mind me saying them back to you when the need arises."

"Okay," I said quietly, but I couldn't return her smile. I thought about the times when I'd punched the arm of our couch while nursing Sam, so I wouldn't punch him in the face instead. No one had ever accused me of being impatient, or having a nasty temper before; now here I was, close to losing it in my therapist's office.

I felt embarrassed and didn't know what else to say, so I looked back down at the carpet. Gail thought for a minute and then asked, "How does it make you feel, Janna, when the baby won't stop crying?"

"Like he's mad at me because I don't know what I'm doing. Like I can't take good care of him. Like I'm a really bad mom or something."

"And how old is your baby, now?"

"About five months."

"Do you have anyone else who helps you with him?"

"Yeah ... my husband, John. Whenever he's not working or going to classes–he's in grad school–he helps."

"But you're home by yourself with Sam most of the time?"

"Yes."

"I see. And how long have you two been married?"

"Almost two years."

"Wow," she breathed out. "Sounds like you've had a lot of change in your life lately, huh?"

"Yeah, I guess so."

"Well, Janna," Gail said, glancing down at the watch on her arm. "I think you're doing a good thing by coming to talk to me about all of this. I can't promise that things are going to suddenly get better after our talk today, but come back and see me again next week and we'll see if we can come up with some strategies to help you feel less angry and less alone."

Those two words, angry and alone, stuck with me throughout the following week, but not in a negative way. They stung, but just a little, sort of like when you pour hydrogen peroxide onto a fresh scrape on your knee. I could imagine tiny bubbles forming on the surface of my heart, so I blew softly toward the redness, and hoped a band aid would be coming soon.

The next time I saw Gail, I wasn't as quiet and shy as I'd been the week before. I sat down and told her many of the bad thoughts that had been running through my mind, which was not at all what I had expected to happen when I made that first appointment. I had figured Gail would do most of the talking and somehow teach me to become a better, more patient mom. Instead, Gail let me do almost all the talking, and she was content to just listen.

My whole life, whenever people would ask me how I was doing, it seemed they never really wanted to know. I grew up in the South, and I was a preacher's daughter, so the place I got asked that question the most was church. Sunday mornings were very busy for the churchgoers I knew, and they didn't make time for heartfelt, lengthy conversation. In that atmosphere, the phrase "How are you?" was more of a greeting than a question. And the proper response to that greeting was one word: "fine." Even if you'd been fighting with your spouse on the way to church. Even if you couldn't stand the person who was asking you. Even if your kids were driving you crazy and you really needed someone to talk to. All we ever told each other was that everything was fine.

Gail gave me the time and space I needed to tell her how I was truly doing. She taught me the freedom of the word "and." As in: I'm a loving mother, and I sometimes lose my temper. Both statements are true. You can be a good parent and still make mistakes. And just because I felt angry when my baby was having a meltdown, it didn't mean I no longer cared about him.

I saw Gail once a week for about three months and she never said to me, "Janna, I think you're clinically depressed." She never gave me an official postpartum diagnosis either. She never treated me like a broken zipper or a dirty sock that needed washing. Instead, she just let me be the non-working, unattractive mess that I was, and she sat with me in the mess, until I learned how to clean myself up and start zipping again.

Gail did tell me once that anger and sadness were two sides of the same coin, which helped me see that just because I wasn't crying all the time, it didn't mean I wasn't depressed—postpartum or otherwise. I understood enough to know that being mad all the time wasn't good for me or my baby, so I worked hard to get rid of my rage. The more I learned to trust Gail, the more I began to tell her about other things that had upset me over the years: times when my mom had told me to smile more, and to "be more bubbly," the pressure I felt from both Mom and Dad to be nearly perfect, as well as the times my parents had punished me too harshly in anger. I didn't want to repeat those behaviors with my little boy. I wanted him to feel like I loved him all the time, no matter what he did or how he acted.

One day I confessed to Gail that I'd always dreamed of becoming a writer. She suggested I begin by writing down the feelings I was having about being a new mom. She encouraged me to buy myself a private journal, and in those moments when it felt like I was losing control, if I could just take a deep breath and remember to go write instead of yell, maybe that would help.

"Your baby's not going to starve to death if you make him wait five minutes to collect yourself," she told me. "And don't be afraid of who might read what you write," she said. "This activity is just for you."

I figured my handwriting was so bad that no one could read it anyway, so I felt free to put all my feelings onto paper, good and bad. I discovered that writing things down felt really good. There was no need to edit or censor myself, I just let everything flow. Once I saw my thoughts written down on paper—caged on the page in black and white, rather than roaming wild in my head—I was able to ferret out the crazy ones, and let go of some of the impossible expectations I'd placed on myself as a new mother and a fairly new wife. After a while, I even began writing letters I knew I would never send, to various people who'd hurt my feelings in the past. The act of turning those feelings and memories into words and sentences freed me from the power they held over me. I was amazed to learn that simple tools, like paper and a pen, could help me learn to control my emotions, rather than let them control me.

I also told Gail about the hurt I felt over all the times we'd moved when I was growing up. Before, I had always told people that moving around a lot had helped me learn how to be more outgoing, and that our family was really close to each other because of all the hard things we'd been through. Those statements were only half true. There's pain involved when you never stay in one town longer than three years, and when people tell you how much they love your dad one day, then yell at him from the pews the next. I trusted Gail with the pain in my little girl heart, and in return she prayed for that little girl to grow up and be healed.

The most effective tools in Gail's therapy box were her simple silence and strong presence. When she did talk, it was mostly to ask me questions that would get me to talk or think a little more. "It's hard for me to believe in God's love sometimes," I admitted one day, "when so many bad things happen in the world ... to me, and to my family."

After that confession she sat quietly for a minute, then suggested I close my eyes. It sounded weird, and at first I resisted, but eventually I relaxed and did what she said. Then Gail asked a stranger than usual question. "Can you tell me where you are?"

"Yeah," I said. "I'm just sitting here on the couch with you." The room was very quiet, and I was sitting very still.

"And what do you see around you?" she asked.

"Nothing." I said. "It's, umm... It's just really dark."

"Can you see anything at all?"

"No," I said.

"Now think a little harder, Janna," her tone was serious. "I want you to tell me everything you can see."

"Well, I'm just sitting here... in the dark..."

Silence.

"Actually, it's more like I'm hunched over, kind of kneeling on the ground."

"And why are you hunched over?"

"I don't know, it's like there's this paved road, or something, underneath my feet. I guess, maybe, I'm bending over to feel it?"

"Can you feel anything else around you?"

"Yeah, there's some kind of wall right next to me. It feels like it's made of bricks ... old and crumbly ones... The edges of the bricks are bumpy, and a little bit sharp."

"What else?"

"It feels damp, and cold."

Gail let me sit with that image for a minute or two. Then she said, "And where is God?"

"Well, I think he's up there somewhere," I raised my hand and pointed up, "but there's another layer of bricks above my head, too." I started to cry.

"It's just so thick," I whispered, "and dark."

"There's no light anywhere. I can't see a way to get out."

* * *

When I was a little girl, I was always the first one in the car when church was over. At the end of every service Dad would call on someone to say the final prayer and while that man was praying, Dad would walk from the pulpit to the back of the church so he could be there waiting to shake hands with everyone as they left the building. Mom usually stayed near the front, to visit with anyone who lingered up there. My little brother usually ran off to play in the churchyard. I don't know where my older sister went, but I didn't care. I was only looking out for myself.

I loved the stillness of our parked car on a hot day, when the fake leather seats burned to the touch. I opened the door, climbed inside and let the quiet heat envelop me. I sat and waited for the rest of my family to be ready to go home, and no one else bothered me. No one shook my hand or said how pretty my dress was. No one asked any embarrassing details about whatever family story Dad had shared as an illustration that day, and best of all, no one told me to smile.

Back then, smiles were just as much a part of your outfit as frilly dresses, white tights, and shiny black shoes. But I couldn't run or climb or jump in those hard shoes, so what was there to smile about? Not to mention all the trouble Mom went to get my hair to look pretty. But guess what happens to nicely styled hair when you run in the churchyard? That's right, it gets all messed up and then you get in trouble for messing up your clothes, too. So, it was better just to go on and sit in the car and wait for some other time to play. A time when you could actually enjoy yourself.

My sister was much better at playing the role of small-town preacher's kid, aka the center of attention, after church was over. She had a pretty singing voice and was often complimented for it. My brother craved the spotlight and was known for silly antics and making everyone laugh. I was just the boring little girl in the middle. Not cute, or funny, or talented. I never caused any trouble, but I also never got noticed for doing anything out of the ordinary, except for being extra quiet. "That girl's always off on some other planet," Mom used to say about me, and while it's true that I could entertain myself for a long time with my dolls and toys, it didn't mean I always liked it that no one ever seemed to worry about me.

For me, the best thing about Sundays came after church, in the form of Sunday dinner. Dinner is what most people think of as the evening meal, but on Sundays, since we went to church again at nighttime, our biggest meal was served at lunchtime and we called it dinner. Mom usually cooked roast beef in the crock pot, along with potatoes, and carrots. We also had dinner rolls, green beans, and some kind of dessert, followed by nearly two hours of silence, while everybody in the house took a nap. We weren't required to sleep once we got older, but we still spent most of the afternoon in our bedrooms, lying on our beds.

It wasn't like I hated everything about church though. I loved singing the hymns. I had most of them memorized and I felt proud that I didn't need to hold a hymnal to read the verses while we sang. Dad's sermons were nice, too. He told great stories and although he got loud on occasion, he was never a judgmental kind of preacher, screaming about "hellfire" and "damnation" all the time. A lot of times he told stories to illustrate his main point, and a lot of times those stories were inspired by the everyday life of our family. Whenever Dad mentioned me in a story, I was embarrassed and happy at the same time. It felt good that Dad paid attention to my little life, but weird that people I didn't really know got to hear all about it. And whenever they asked me questions about it later on, I never knew what to say to their smiling faces. It always felt like they were teasing me, even though they were probably just being curious.

When I was five years old I decided I wanted to become a Christian and I was always asking Mom and Dad when it would be my turn to walk down the aisle, pray the prayer, and accept Jesus into my heart. They gave me short answers like "soon" and "whenever you're ready," but they weren't sure if I really was ready, so they waited and watched, hoping for me to do something special that showed I understood what it meant to make such a big decision.

But for me it never felt like a decision because I never chose to believe in something. I don't remember not knowing that Jesus had died for me. I don't remember not knowing that I was a sinner who needed saving. I don't remember not knowing about heaven and hell. I only remember believing what I had always known, what I'd been taught from infancy: that death was real and hell was imminent, unless I placed my faith in Jesus Christ, the one who came to set us all free.

One night when we were living in Winter Haven, Florida, my sister and I were fighting with each other instead of going to sleep at bedtime. We shared a room as well as a full-size canopy bed. I have no idea what the fight was about, but I remember that the lights had already been turned off, and we'd already been warned to get to sleep. The crack of light from the hallway grew bigger as Dad opened the door, got me out of bed, and carried me to the bathroom for a spanking. But after he walked me over to the toilet, Dad told me to sit down instead of bend over. Then he crouched down beside me and started asking me questions about what happened. Finally, he asked if I understood that staying up and fighting was disobedience, and disobedience was a sin. I told him yes. Then Dad asked me if I wanted Jesus to forgive me for that sin and to come into my heart and save me–from all the sin that I'd ever committed, and all the sin that I would continue to commit as long as I was alive.

"Yes," I told him. "I do." So, Dad led me in a simple prayer of salvation, hugged my neck, and told me he was proud of me. Then he put me back to bed.

The next morning Dad and I were walking out to the car so he could take me to school. There in the parking lot, with the parsonage beside us and the church right behind us, Dad asked if I remembered what had happened the night before. "Yes, sir," I said. Then he asked if it still felt real to me. "Yes, sir," I said. That's as much as I can recall about the momentous event. We never wrote down the date or what day of the week it was, but Mom and Dad both say it was in November, just a few weeks before I turned six.

Mom and Dad made me wait a few more months to get baptized. They wanted to make sure I was serious first, and when they finally let me Dad of course did the dunking. Every preacher has his own way of baptizing. Dad's custom has always been to put his hand out in front of the person he is about to baptize, just before taking him or her under the water. Then the person getting baptized is supposed to grab onto Dad's forearm with both hands, while Dad plugs the man or woman's nose with his thumb and knuckled forefinger, and plunges him or her "beneath the cleansing flood." Some ministers like to put a white cloth in the hand they extend, so the baptized can expect a certain degree of separation between the minister's hand and his or her nose. Not my Dad though. My Dad is a bare nose grabber.

I'm sure we practiced at home before my official baptism ceremony, but when it came time for me to grab Dad's forearm that day in the water, I panicked. I reached up for the back of his neck instead, and held on for dear life. Clearly, Dad never saw this coming or he would have stopped me somehow. Still, he was a professional, and he only paused for half a second before deciding to just go down into the water with me. This would never have worked on another grown-up, but since I was a child and he was a former state champion quarterback, he was able to get me covered without completely dousing his own head. I'm sure there was applause when we both resurfaced, but I don't remember it. I'm sure people told me how proud they were afterwards, and I'm sure Mom took pictures and I was embarrassed. I don't remember any of that though. What I remember is grabbing my Dad's ample neck and lacing my fingers behind it. I remember not letting go.

When I began therapy sixteen years later, my faith in God looked much the same. I had a primal belief in God, but it felt like my faith was wholly dependent on how well I could hold onto God myself. So much life had happened since that initial dunking that Jesus felt far away and incompetent, perhaps even impotent. I knew I was supposed to love God with all my heart. I'd heard over and over again about the sacrifice he'd made to show the world his love. But that's how he feels about everyone, I thought. Isn't there something more specific, I wondered, that he only feels for me?

Growing up in church, I'd heard many people talk about having a "personal relationship with Jesus Christ," but I didn't know what that really felt like. I knew right from wrong, and I'd been trying to do the right things my whole life. Yet, it felt like all I got for my trouble was more and more disappointment. More pain, more fear. I'd read oodles of devotionals over the years and I'd practiced daily quiet times during several different phases of my life, but I knew I didn't mean it when we sang songs like "Oh, How I love Jesus," and "Christ Is All I Need." No, what I felt instead were my own slippery wet knuckles, and I wasn't sure how much longer they could hold on.

The place where Gail and I attended church was in the repurposed store of a strip mall. We both had friends in the band that played for half an hour every Sunday. Then the pastor would walk up on stage and share a simple Bible story. It was a hip little place, back when contemporary worship services were just beginning to sprout up across the country. Since we'd both grown up in the Baptist world of the deep South, John and I found flip-flops and rock music far more appealing than singing hymns and dressing to impress on Sunday mornings.

One of our pastor's favorite sayings at that time was this: worship is transformational. He taught us that when you gave your time and attention to praising God, the Holy Spirit was free to do his work in your heart. I'm not sure whether I believed him, or if I just liked the music, but Sunday after Sunday I stood and sang with all my heart. Even when I was exhausted from caring for my newborn baby, even though I was struggling with some of the feelings that had surfaced through my counseling sessions with Gail, the truths that were shared in that place, and the loving people there, compelled me to sing.

One morning after his talk, the pastor called the band back up to the stage. I have no idea what the message was about that day, but I can tell you what happened to me during that final singing.

The room was dimly lit, but my eyes were closed anyhow. And the music was loud, because that's how we liked it. I think we were singing "Let the River Flow" and I think my hands were halfway raised, more out of surrender than devotion. That's when it happened. In my head, in the vision of my imagination, I saw a bright yellow light. I looked up to see bricks falling away and a man on a horse breaking them apart with a shining silver lance. It sounds cheesy, but he was wearing a suit of armor, like some knight from the middle ages. Suddenly, I knew the man was Jesus. He found me stuck inside that old brick tunnel, scared and alone in the dark. He knew I couldn't bust out of there myself; so he came and broke through instead. And he did all of that, just for me. Because he saw me, because he knew all about me, and he still loved me anyway. All at once, I felt surrounded by God's unique and perfect love. For once, there was no room left for fear.

It surprised me so much that I nearly fell over, but I managed to open my eyes and sit back down in my cushiony seat first. But after a minute I had to stand up again because I was crying so hard that I made noise, and I'm not the kind of person who is inappropriately loud in church. Locked behind a stall door in the bathroom, tears continued to pour as I tried to catch my breath; then I heard someone else open the main door. I peeked out and saw Gail, so I unlocked the stall and almost tackled her with a hug. It took her a minute to figure out what was going on. I was a slobbering mess who wasn't making much sense as I tried to explain it to her. Finally, I said that it was a good cry and I was actually feeling happy inside. "Oh," she said, sounding surprised and bewildered as she patted my back and tried to steady my shaking shoulders.

Once I regained a normal breathing pattern, Gail let me go. She backed up, opened her purse and dug around in the bottom of it for a few seconds. "Here," she said as she pulled out her hand and offered me a cinnamon-flavored Altoid. "It'll dam up the deluge," she promised.

It was another awkward moment, me with my red, wet face and her with her giant purse full of surprises. Even though I couldn't explain it very well to her, it's important that Gail came into the restroom at that moment. She was the only one I'd ever talked to about that cold, dark tunnel, the only one who could understand the miracle that had just happened. For the first time in my life, I got it! I didn't have to dig my own way out. It had never been up to me in the first place. Just because my arms were wrapped around Jesus' neck, my fingers tangled in his hair, my hands clutched tightly together, it didn't mean that I was the one doing the holding. I hadn't been able to see it before, but Jesus had always been holding me, too.

The next time I met with Gail I tried to explain myself more clearly, though I've often wondered if I ever made any sense to her at all. How much can we really see inside the heart of another human being anyhow? No one can say for sure, but I'm so thankful that she tried. For what could be more holy than becoming a witness? Than caring enough about the pain of someone else to sit long with them and listen? To risk feeling someone else's hurt yourself, in order to help their hurt begin to heal.

Talk therapy with Gail was my first step toward healing, from what I would later recognize as postpartum depression, but it was also something more. For the first time in my life, it felt like Jesus came down to earth and put on human skin, just for me, little Janna Beth Young Barber. But it wasn't the skin of a newborn baby this time. It was the skin of a forty-two-year-old housewife, recently turned social worker, named Gail Walker.

All these years later, my memory of those days can feel a little blurry around the edges, but when I quiet myself, I can still remember the sound of breaking bricks. I can feel the warmth of being held by someone who knows me a little too well, and loves me anyway. I see the brightness of a blinding, yet comforting light. I smell the heat of my own perspiration, and in my mouth I taste the strong, sweet flavor of cinnamon.

Notley Road

2000

When Sam was eight months old, our financial situation required us to make a big change. John quit grad school and began looking for a full-time job, one that paid more than his part time job at the bookstore. John's dad heard about a job at the company where he worked in Baltimore, and we ended up moving a thousand miles away to the state of Maryland. Not only did I experience culture shock in this move from the deep South to the not-so-South, it was also the first time I'd ever lived so far away from my family. The first time I 'd need the help of an airplane to get back home again.

In April we found a duplex just right for our family. It had an office, two bedrooms, one bath, a kitchen, and a family room. The strangest part of the house was its lack of a laundry room. Instead, the washer and dryer were lined up against the wall on the left side of the kitchen. Convenient, but not exactly ideal. When people came to visit, I pointed it out before they had the chance to comment on it, hoping the imperfection would be less noticeable. I'm not sure it ever worked.

I worked hard to keep our little house clean back then. The dishes were always washed, and the laundry always got put away. I spent my days taking care of Sam, going to the grocery store, and doing housework. I got out of the house one or two times a week, either for a playdate, or to go to a Mom's group. When Sam napped in the afternoons, I sometimes napped with him, but usually I took advantage of the quiet to read whatever book my other mom friends were reading or catch up on the chores that had fallen behind.

One day I bought a new tablecloth for our vintage kitchen table–the one John and I found at a barn in the middle of nowhere, just a few months after we got married. The tabletop was ceramic, and hand painted, with sage green trim and an ivory background. The legs were delicately carved and stained, and there was a hidden drawer in the middle that I imagined filling with funky antique silverware someday.

The tablecloth I bought came from Walmart. It was vinyl, with textured cotton cloth on the back, that helped it cling to the slick surface of the table, and not slide off every time you wiped it down. The problem with the tablecloth was that I didn't like the pattern on it. When I first saw it, I figured the low price meant I didn't need to like it very much. It accomplished its purpose after all, protecting the table and catching all the spills. But the bright blue checks and fire red cherries matched neither my curtains nor my mood on most days, and no matter how often I smoothed it out, the plastic kept wrinkling up on me. So, one day I just stopped using it, and eventually, I threw it out.

In the middle of adjusting to a new town, a new house and a new job, we began to figure out who we were as a family, without the influence of either of our parents. For the first time we were facing real parenting decisions on our own and we found ourselves asking lots of questions. Questions like: Do we discipline Sam when he doesn't obey? How should we go about that? Does time out work? How do we feel about spanking? Should we put Sam in preschool? Do we really need to sit down to dinner as a family every single night? How much time should we spend together and what do we most want our child to know? Like the vintage table and the cheap tablecloth, we had to decide what was worth holding onto and what was okay to toss out.

The church we found in Pasadena was a small plant called New Hope.

They met on Saturday nights in the auditorium of an elementary school. The pastor called it "church in a truck" because every weekend they had to unload all the chairs and sound equipment from the back of a moving van, where they stored everything during the week.

The pastor's name was Ron and he was originally from Indiana. He was a short, stocky man with a nose that did not betray his Roman heritage. He spoke in a soft, lilting rhythm, with a raspy voice and a midwestern accent, and when he preached you got the sense he needed his message just as much as the people listening to him.

One night, Ron preached a sermon about forgiveness, and it was unlike any I'd ever heard before. He read from a passage in Matthew 18, where Jesus told a parable about an unforgiving servant. I was familiar with the passage and thought I understood the instruction behind it. But Ron challenged my thinking as the sermon came to a close.

Isn't it crazy that this man, this man who had just been told that he didn't owe the king any money at all, went out and demanded his servant to give him all the money he owed him, immediately?

Just picture it, Ron said. Let's say you were two months late on your rent and your landlord said to you, "It's ok, man, you don't owe me for this month, or last month. In fact, you never have to pay me rent anymore for the rest of your life."

If he told you that you didn't owe him any money at all, that your debt was completely cancelled, would your first reaction be to go over to your neighbor's house and grab him by the neck and yell at him to give you back the $50 you'd loaned him six months ago?

No, that's crazy, right?

The only thing that would make you do that, is if somehow you thought you still had to pay your landlord. If you believed that you still owed him all that money, that's when you would start trying to collect.

But if you only realized just how much debt you had that didn't have to be paid anymore...

Then you'd never ask another person for another penny.

* * *

Not long after Dad baptized me in Florida, our family moved again, this time to Arkansas. Dad's parents were living in Hot Springs, in the house he'd helped his Dad build when he was just sixteen. Mom's parents were still together then, living in Oklahoma, so the move was our attempt to get back closer to extended family–close enough to drive over for a long weekend or part of summer vacation.

The place we settled in was West Memphis, one of the larger cities in Arkansas, nestled just west of the Tennessee border and only thirty minutes from Elvis' Graceland. Dad pastored a church called Heritage Baptist, and the church housed a Christian school which my sister and I both attended. She was in fourth grade when she started and I was in first, but after a few months I was reading so well the teacher and principal asked my parents if they wanted to move me over a few rows so I could join the second graders. Mom and Dad were excited for their little genius. "Sure, she can!" they told the school. "We think it's a great idea!" they said to me.

When you're a girl growing up in the south, being smart is never as good as being pretty, no matter what Gilbert Blythe says. But I grabbed onto it anyhow. Nothing else was coming my way and people were visibly impressed when Dad told stories about me, already reading from The King James Bible. From that point on, until I graduated high school, whenever I met someone new and they asked me how old I was, I always followed up my numerical answer with, "and I'm in third grade, but I should only be in second because I skipped first grade!" The age and the grade went up year after year, but the part about me being a smarty-pants stayed the same. And finally, it was a story I could tell for myself.

When I say I wasn't a pretty little girl, I'm not trying to get you to feel sorry for me, I'm just stating facts. I was the second born daughter to a statuesque beauty whose wavy blonde hair, coffee brown eyes, and mocha colored skin were next to perfect; but I looked like my Dad. I'm not saying I was ugly, some people even said I was cute, but nobody called me pretty. And my mother wasn't just nice looking, she was gorgeous. "You're too pretty to be a pastor's wife," is a statement she heard from several different congregations. She's over sixty years old now, and still one of the most beautiful women I know.

From day one, Mom tried to get my hair to do something other than just lay flat and straight on my head. She used honey or Karo syrup, whichever was handy, to shape my fine black hair into a single ringlet; then she stuck a tiny pink bow on top. I've got the pictures to prove it. Years later, I slept with my hair in sponge curlers, or else I wore it up in braids and ponytails, but wearing my dark brown locks straight and stringy just irritated Mom—which was of course, how I preferred to wear it. Pierced ears on young girls were frowned upon by some conservatives in the congregation, but anything else she could get away with to make me look feminine and pretty was allowed, and she took full advantage of them all. Ruffled bloomers and lacy socks, shiny patent leather shoes and can-cans; I was her own little angel, a perfect doll. So, what if I didn't have the face for it? Who cared about the blotchy red birthmark beneath my right eye, or my endless supply of freckles? Mom would make me look cute in spite of my lackluster hair and gap-toothed smile. She was always up for a challenge.

Looking the part was important to Mom, and the singular life lesson she meant to impart to her children was this: It doesn't matter how you feel on the inside, so long as you look happy on the outside. She was a second-generation Pastor's wife and knew instinctively what it took to impress people. Her mother had taught her that what matters absolutely, more than anything, is what the congregation might think. So, you were always supposed to look your best, and you were always supposed to have a smile on your face. Your house should be clean and inviting, with a pitcher of sweet tea in the fridge in case company comes over unexpectedly. This was how you helped other people learn to love Jesus. First, they would see how perfect your life was, and then they would begin to want that life for themselves. Or else she just wanted the people at church to like her so they wouldn't send Dad packing sometime in the next year. That might have been her main motivation after all. Either way, she played her part like a pro.

I can't speak for Mom, but the pressure of looking and acting perfect all the time was stressful for me. I did an okay job of hiding that stress most of the time. People tended to think I was quiet and shy, and while I can be both those things quite a lot, I was mainly scared. By the time I graduated high school, the longest we had lived anywhere was three and a half years, so my greatest fear growing up was having to move again, and I was constantly terrified. Every time Mom and Dad said we needed to have a family meeting; I knew what they were going to say: Time to say goodbye to all your friends. Time to pack up everything you own. Time to see how much of your heart is left to take with us.

When I was in fourth grade, I decided I wanted to be a cheerleader. We'd moved twice since West Memphis and ended up in a small town in northwest Arkansas called Greenwood. There were only three thousand people living in this rural farming community, with only one school and four or five churches. The county had a well-run recreational league though and nearly every kid participated in one sport or another.

Mom was a cheerleader when she was in high school and Dad played football, and Mom loved pointing out that she still cheered him on as a preacher. I'd never been interested in anything else Mom liked, so she was excited we finally had something to do together. In fact, she volunteered to coach my squad. But instead of bringing us closer together, her coaching drove me further away. Mom had high expectations for us. Sure, we were only cheering for elementary flag football, but that wouldn't stop us from being the best squad in the league. We practiced and practiced and practiced. Mom taught us dance routines set to the music of the Beach Boys. She helped us build pyramids and taught me how to do jumps, kicks, and cartwheels. I didn't have very good form though and she was forever pushing me to do better.

"No spaghetti arms, Janna. Lock those elbows into place!"

"You've got scarecrow fingers again, honey. Pay attention to your hands!"

"Make it pop, Janna! I know you can do better than that."

I wasn't sure I could though, and eventually I stopped trying. I just wanted to wear a cute skirt and have fun with my friends, so I continued to disappoint Mom and she continued to push me harder. But it wasn't just cheerleading anymore. Soon It became what clothes and shoes I wore to school, how well I curled my bangs and whether or not I remembered to put on lipstick. I began to feel like she was no longer talking to me, but at me. And like a pink birthmark that turns red after too many hours in the sun, the more she picked on me, the meaner I became.

It started with something very small. Instead of calling her Momma, like my siblings and I had done our whole lives, I began to call her Mom. Instead of saying "Okay, Momma," when she asked me to set the table for dinner, I began to whine: "What are we having Mo-om? Why spaghetti again, Mom? How come I have to clean my room, Mom?" Then in junior high, it changed to Mother, as in, "Why should I have to put away the dishes, Mother? It's not like the President's coming over to our house for dessert today. And finally, when I was a senior in high school, I tried to get away with calling her woman, as in "What did you do with my tennis shoes, woman?" That one didn't go over too well with Dad, but it didn't stop me from trying, as often as I could, to push her many, many buttons.

Like most mother/daughter relationships, ours grew to be complicated. Mom knew what it was like for me, to have to move all the time, to grow up in a preacher's house, living in small towns in the south. But she also felt like she could help things turn out right, and better, for our family. She would be a different kind of mother than her Mom was. She wouldn't quit on her husband when the times got tough. Her faith was stronger, and more real than that. She would make sure everything was as it should be for her family; that we were all perfect.

So, she taught me to dress and act a certain way. She encouraged me to be sweet and outgoing, but to me it felt like criticism, and not the constructive kind. And it was more than wishing I was prettier. This was about who I was. Mom was an extrovert, a high energy person who saw a problem and fixed it, a creative, determined woman, never content to sit still and just breathe. There was always something that needed to be cleaned, pressed or mended. Always some different person to talk to, some new recipe to try, some exciting project to tackle. I, on the other hand, craved routine. I was content to eat the same meals day in and day out, to walk slowly home from school, to sit and daydream all afternoon, to not talk for hours on end. In short, Mom was a rabbit and I was a turtle. But it felt more like she thought I was a slow bunny, who needed a good kick in the pants.

The thing about turtles is the more that you mess with them, the more they withdraw. So, I just curled up in my shell and decided I didn't need Mom anymore. I still had Dad to help out with things like driving me to basketball practice and making me laugh. Mom became the lady who cooked and cleaned and bought me stuff. I didn't need anything else from her and it helped to have one simple target for all my anger about moving and having to make new friends over and over again. Soon Dad became the hero of my childhood and Mom turned into the evil stepmother, whether or not she deserved it.

I've read since that this psychological phenomenon is not so uncommon in childhood. It's probably where the evil stepmother notion came from in the first place. Author Anne Lammot says she tied her invisible umbilical cord to her father's ankle when she was a little girl, following the example her mom had given her, because it gave them both the "illusion of power and connection." But just because daughters do this, it doesn't mean their mothers are actual villains. I know because I have a daughter myself now, one who's more like her Daddy than me most of the time. Who calls me Mom instead of Momma, like she did when she was little. Who questions most of my actions on a daily basis. She's doing the hard work of growing up and becoming her own woman and I'm learning how to be able to let her go.

* * *

The summer after we moved to Maryland, I began meeting with Ron for more counseling since Gail and I hadn't been able to finish our sessions when we moved. One day in his office Ron asked me to pull out my driver's license. I got it out and handed it across the desk to him. He took it and looked at it for a minute. Then he looked up at me.

"Is that you?" he asked, pointing to the image in the corner.

"Yeah," I said. "That's me."

"Really?" he asked.

"I mean it's a picture from last year," I explained.

"Oh, I know that," he said. "But what I'm asking is whether or not it's really you?"

"Of course it's me!" I said. "Who else would it be?"

"So, you're telling me that this picture," he said, holding it up in the air. "This little square that I'm pointing at right here–that's who you are?"

"Well, no," I admitted. "Not when you put it like that."

"Yeah," he said kind of smugly. "I didn't think so."

I waited.

"This picture right here. That's just an image of you, right? Well, so is this idea you still carry around about yourself as a kid. That's not who you are anymore, Janna, and you don't have to keep trying to be that perfect little girl anymore."

I didn't believe it at first. Of course, I had to be perfect. Dad was still preaching, and I was still his daughter, wasn't I? Wouldn't it continue to be that way for the rest of my life? It was so hard to imagine myself any differently. I'd always been the quiet, respectful girl who kept her true feelings hidden. The one who did what needed to be done and tried to help keep the peace while the rest of the world turned and turned and turned. The one who worried about everything, but said nothing. There was no way I could start speaking up now; and besides that, who would listen?

It took several months to sink in, but eventually I decided it was worth it to redefine myself. It was hard work to think of myself as more than just a preacher's daughter, but I began to realize that I didn't need to worry about Dad getting fired anymore. It was no longer in my power to control what happened with his job. In fact, it never had been up to me in the first place. It also didn't matter what Mom might think about the clothes I wore or how clean I kept my house. The friends I had now didn't see me as just a goody-two shoes who knew everything there was to know about God and religion. And the people I sat next to in church, believe it or not, had not come there in order to find fault with me.

Slowly, slowly, my vision began to change. Now I was a wife and a mother. I'd gone off to college and graduated with a degree all on my own. I was a grown woman, I could behave however I wanted, and the only one responsible for that behavior was me. I was a good friend; I had other good friends who knew me and loved me, just as I was. I was a child of God, the God who cared about my pain and longed to heal me. The God who knew my hopes and fears: that I wanted to be a writer and to stop being so scared all the time. But most importantly, I was a work in progress. And I had the rest of my life to keep on becoming, whoever it was I most wanted to be in the end. Because it's not the life we're born into that dictates who we become. It's our own decisions that we make, day after day, after day.

When it came time to decorate the house for Christmas that year, I bought some oranges and a can of cloves for Sam and me to decorate together. It was a tradition Mom had taught us when we were kids. She took some bright plaid ribbon and wrapped it around the oranges and tied it off so they could hang from the ceiling in the kitchen. Then she sat us at the table with bowls of cloves and told us to push them into the skin of the oranges. Sometimes I made a pattern and sometimes I drove the cloves in randomly. It was a job that got easier the older we got, as smaller, softer fingers don't work so well when pressing prickly bits of wood into a tough orange rind. But a spicy citrus aroma filling up your house in the dead of winter is well worth the time and effort it takes to produce this decorative air freshener.

As I helped Sam with his orange I began to think about my relationship with my Mom. Just because we had a rough time in the past didn't mean it had to be that way forever. Ron and Gail helped me realize that I'd been holding onto an idealized notion of what mothers looked like, and that perfect mold was one that neither my mom, nor I, could ever fit. They encouraged me to let go of those old ideals. It was time to accept my mother, and myself, for who we really were, the prickly bits as well as the sweet scents.

So, I decided to write Mom a letter. I sat down at the kitchen table by the window one afternoon and began scratching out my thoughts on an old legal pad. It was a cloudy spring day and the ceramic was cool when I laid my forehead on the table to think.

"The truth might hurt initially," Gail had taught me, "but it never creates any lasting harm." So, I admitted to Mom that I'd been mad at her for several years. "I knew that you loved me," I wrote, "but because you were often critical, I began to believe that you didn't really like me too much."

Initially, Mom was hurt; and at first, she didn't even acknowledge my letter, so I wondered if it got lost in the mail. But a few months later we had the first of many healing conversations.

We were standing in the kitchen of her house in Colorado, where Mom and Dad had moved a few months after John and I came to Maryland. The sun was shining warm and bright outside, but inside Mom's kitchen it felt dark and cool. Sam and I had come to visit for a week that summer and everyone else was at work, except for the three of us and her Dad, who was downstairs taking a nap.

Mom had recently become the primary caretaker for her Dad, recently diagnosed with Alzheimer's disease. Papaw John was getting harder to handle. He would go for long walks and end up getting lost. In the evenings, he had spells where he became paranoid and accused Mom, Dad, and my brother of trying to hurt him or steal his stuff. Mom did the best she could by him, but it was hard for her to see her own father behaving like a confused child. He'd also become verbally abusive, even when he was in his right mind. That afternoon he'd just finished chewing her out for not folding his t-shirts properly.

Mom told me how frustrating it was to try and please him.

"I just can't seem to do anything that's good enough for him," she said. "Not the laundry or the cooking. He doesn't even like the music I play for him on the piano." Then, she stopped talking for a minute, put down her dish towel and looked straight at me.

"I guess you know how that feels, huh?"

The gear switch happened so suddenly that I didn't catch on at first, but as she stood there waiting for me to answer I realized what she was getting at. It wasn't the first time she'd admitted being too hard on me, but for the first time in a very long time, her words sank into the pillow of my heart, without bouncing off.

"I know what you mean, Mom," I finally answered. "But I'm sure that Papaw loves you very much, and he really does appreciate all that you do for him. Even if he's not very good at showing it to you right now."

Later that night I was lying in bed when I heard Jesus tell me that he was my new landlord. He said I didn't owe him any money to live in his house, so there was no need to collect any money from Mom. Our relationship was not repaired in that instant, like some picture-perfect moment in the movies. It took a while to stop treating Mom like she still owed me something. I had to start reminding myself, every time I remembered a harsh word that stung me. Those words were just little cheap coins, paper dollar bills clenched tightly in my fist, that I didn't need to spend anymore. Jesus was not standing there waiting for me to turn around and give that money to him, so it was okay to let all those small debts go.

Once I loosened my grip and the bad memories began to slide out, I started remembering more of the good things about Mom. Like the times I saw her in the mornings drinking coffee, still dressed in her velvet purple robe, sitting in a rocking chair, reading her Bible. The times I heard her sing in church. I remembered how she wrapped her tired arms around me time and time again. I tasted the food of love and life that she served me, how she kept on putting all of us kids first. I remembered the softness of her lips against my cheek as she kissed me goodnight. Her love for me had been real after all. Over and over again, she cooked, cleaned and held our little family together the best she could–while Dad faced one church turmoil after another.

When we were kids Mom used to tell us this story, about a mom who loved her little boy so much that she tucked him in every night, for his whole life, even when he grew up and moved away from home. The mother in the story always sang this one song over and over for her son and when Mom got to that part in the story, she'd sing her own version of the song to us. After Sam was born someone gave us a book that tells the same story. It's called Love You Forever, and every time I read it, I hear my mother's alto voice singing that melody. It's a great memory to have back on my good side, the memory of me in mom's lap, as she sits in her rocking chair, humming, until we both fall asleep.

I'll love you forever

I'll like you for always

As long as I'm living,

My mommy you'll be.

The grace we've been shown only begets more grace. The forgiveness Jesus gives me for not being perfect frees me up to let others be imperfect as well. Others like my Mom, who was only ever guilty of doing the best she could. Once I realized that, I sought to make amends by writing her a letter admitting my resentment. It wasn't what she wanted to hear at first and if I could do it over again, I would try to say it more graciously. But it was the best I could do at the time. It's not easy work to transform a mother-daughter relationship into one where we're both sisters in Christ. I'm sure I'll have a hard time getting used to it myself one day, when my own daughter stops being the little girl in the silver picture frame on my desk and begins walking away, down the road toward her one true image.

Notley Road

2002

On the evening of March 3, 2002, I was at church. I was wearing a green t-shirt, blue jeans and a silver cross necklace my sister had given me for Christmas. Tears were falling down my cheeks, but I had a great smile on my face. "Thank you, Lord, for your mercies," I prayed.

I had taken a pregnancy test before church that morning, the third one, because the two from the night before were so faint. And it was positive. After eleven months of trying, eleven months of possibility followed by disappointment; finally, there was a plus sign. I was overcome with joy, already dreaming of a baby. Maybe it would be a girl this time. She would be born in November, just like me. How amazing. I stood and clapped my hands as we all sang a song called "Sweet Mercies."

After church, we went to a birthday dinner for one of our friends and John accidentally let the cat out of the bag. Suddenly, everyone knew, and they were all so excited for us. "Praise the Lord!" they said. "Thank you, Jesus," I thought.

On Monday evening we met with a realtor to sign paperwork on the new house we were buying. On Tuesday morning, I lost the baby.

The morning I miscarried. I called my friend Maureen. She had twin babies who were about a year younger than my son Sam. She'd had a difficult time getting pregnant with them, and I knew she'd lost at least one baby before. When she picked up the phone I said, "I think I might be having a ..." but I couldn't get the word "miscarriage" to come out of my mouth. It felt strange and clumsy on my tongue, like a foreign word with rolling "r"s that I could never pronounce.

> *Miscarriage: A three syllable word that sounds like you dropped something because you didn't know how to carry it.*

That couldn't be what was happening to me. No, that word was just a sterile diagnosis, something you heard mentioned at prayer time back when you were in high school. So, your small group prayed for somebody's aunt Lisa, and then you went right back to talking about the cute new guy in church this morning. That word didn't match up with what I was going through. Only eight hours before, I'd gone to sleep with a baby growing inside me. Then when I woke up, there was a drop of her blood on my panties. Surely there was another word for this experience.

Once Maureen figured out what I'd been trying to say, she told me she was so sorry. She tried her best to comfort me, but I couldn't come up with a coherent response. Finally, she suggested I call my doctor, and John, of course. I hung up the phone, stood in my kitchen, and waited for something familiar to happen.

A fresh, new life was literally slipping out of my body and there was nothing I could do about it? It was the most difficult thing I'd ever tried to comprehend. I was in shock. My mind flashed back to a morning six months earlier, when John called to tell me that he was coming home from work in Baltimore at 9:30 on a Tuesday morning. "Turn on the TV," he said, and I spent the next hour on the couch with Sam, waiting for John's car to pull up, glued in front of the worst moving picture we'd ever seen.

John and I spent most of the afternoon at the doctor's office, while Sam went to grandma's. When I got home, I took a long nap. When I woke up, I thought it might be good to get out of the house for a while. One of our church friends had planned a ladies' spa night for several of us, scheduled to start at eight. Maybe being with other people would be better than sitting alone in a swirl of bad thoughts. When I got there, it was a little awkward for the women who, by then, had heard about what happened. They seemed surprised to see me, but I tried to brush it off. I didn't want to think about being sad anymore. I wanted to play games, laugh, and tell jokes. A few hours later I'd nearly forgotten about that morning. I was relaxed and feeling good, not thinking of anything but the present moment. That's when someone said her sister's birthday was in November and she needed some ideas on how to plan a big surprise party for her.

I was jolted back to reality with that one sentence. I gasped but couldn't exhale; I was afraid tears would follow my breath. I didn't want to ruin my friend's party with my sadness, and I couldn't stand the thought of everyone turning their attention on me. I had to get out of there and I had to do it now. Hillary, the girl who drove me to the party was a new friend, but already we felt close. She noticed me losing composure and quietly asked if I was ready to leave.

When we got to my house I didn't want to go in yet. It was late and the windows were dark, so I knew John and Sam were already asleep. I didn't have the courage to enter a quiet, empty house so I asked Hillary an open-ended question in order to stall. In the middle of her story I started crying. Hillary looked over at me and teared up as well. Then she began to tell me all the details she remembered from the day she'd had her own miscarriage.

"It's probably the suckiest thing that's ever happened to me," she said. Then she gave me some advice.

"You're always gonna miss your baby, Janna. You're always gonna wonder about him or her and it's always gonna suck that you never got to meet that baby," she said. "But it won't always hurt this bad. And the one good thing that might come out of this is that one day, maybe you'll be able to be there for somebody else when it happens to them. Just like I'm here for you now."

It was just the right thing to say, and I knew she meant it. Then she hugged me, and I got out of the car.

That conversation could've been a jump start toward healing, but I wasn't ready to drive there yet. I was still numb, still shellshocked, still hoping I'd wake up in the morning and this day would all be some bad dream. There

I was, a young mother with years of pain behind me. I had no idea there were still so many hard days ahead.

We sang the "Sweet Mercies" song through the rest of that Spring and into summer, and every time it began, I would catch my breath. It felt as if each chord change cracked a new fracture in the middle of my heart; I couldn't sing the words out loud anymore. In fact, I wasn't able to sing most of the songs at church. For about two months, church services were the hardest part of my week. It took me nearly two hours to get ready because I felt like I had to look perfect. I had to have the perfect hairstyle, one that said, "Don't worry about me." Then I needed to apply my makeup perfectly so people would know not to ask any embarrassing questions. And finally, I tried to wear perfect clothes, outfits that told everyone, "No, really, my heart's not broken anymore."

Of course, it was all a big lie, and I ended up crying during worship time, week after week, but not too much. I never let myself go completely, and I may have even looked spiritual to some people.

I might have even been "spiritual" in the fact that I never got mad at God during that time. Somehow, I sensed that He was just as heartbroken as me. It was all the other people at church who drove me crazy though. They'd stare down at me with tilted heads, and sympathetic looks in their eyes.

"How are you doing?" they'd ask.

"We're praying for you," they'd say.

But all I wanted was to be left alone. Then there were a few numbskulls who said some really dumb things. Things like: "Well, God's timing is perfect," and "The good news is that you can still get pregnant." I tried to fake what I supposed they wanted to hear, but a few times I was stunned to silence when I remembered some of those same shallow platitudes coming out of my own mouth. I was guilty of being a numbskull myself.

I mostly isolated myself, justifying my withdrawal with this thought: "They've never been through anything like this, what do they know?"

It wasn't true though. Plenty of people I knew had endured painful circumstances, but I wanted someone to say the right thing, to give me an answer for what had happened to me, and why. I didn't understand yet that what I needed was for someone to hug me, for someone to be there and listen to me while I cried and cried. What I needed was to cry and cry. Instead I felt this internal pressure to appear normal. "Everyone else has problems, too," I thought, "and most of them are tougher than mine." So, I decided to just pretend like everything was going fine. I overheard my husband tell someone on the phone one night, "She's taking it pretty well."

"Sounds like I've got him fooled," I said to myself, "surely everyone else is, too."

A few months before I got pregnant, I began working part-time as a caterer. On evenings and weekends, I put on a bow tie, tuxedo shirt, and a pair of black pants. Then I went to work at a historic mansion that housed both a restaurant and a party tent, for weddings and other important events. After the miscarriage, I loved escaping to this place where no one knew what had happened and I could just blend in and focus on my tasks. I wasn't close with any of the people I worked with, so I hadn't told them about being pregnant or losing the baby. At the job we only talked about the job; we knew virtually nothing about each other, aside from what happened on site.

The ride home always got to me though. It'd be late at night and it took all the strength I had not to pull into some local bar, which I'd purposely driven by, even though I'd never gotten drunk before. For the first time ever, I thought seriously about getting a tattoo. I felt like I needed something to dull my pain. But then when people asked me about it, what would I tell them: "These are the initials of my dead daughter?" Talk about a conversation killer.

One night I drove past our church office, and saw a light still shining in the second story window. It was Ron, up late studying for his next sermon. I parked my car and went up to see him, and for the first time, I really let myself cry. He hugged me and made me a cup of coffee. Then he told me to cry some more. I told him about some of the insensitive things people had said to me, and how mad they'd made me feel. He assured me that those people really loved me. "Unfortunately, they're just not very wise with their words," he said.

Ron told me that he didn't have any answers for all the questions I had about my baby. Questions like: Why did God let this happen to me? Does God know if my baby was a boy or a girl, and what does an embryo look like up in heaven anyhow? Is it a baby, or just a soul, floating around in a tiny little bubble?

"No one has the answers to all those questions, Janna," he said, looking at me from behind his desk. "But I've got a feeling you'll know who your baby is when you get there, hon."

That made me cry some more, so he waited and handed me a box of tissues.

"Maybe you should start asking some different questions, Janna." He shifted in his seat and picked up a pen from his desk. "Ask yourself if you still think God is good? Do you think maybe he still loves you, even though he's allowed this painful thing to happen to you? Do you think you can ever learn to trust Him again?"

One day, a few weeks later, I was spending time alone with my journal again, when I began to understand something important. I sat at my kitchen table and imagined Jesus sitting in the chair across from me. I pictured myself asking him a question, "Why did you give me a baby, only to take it away?" When I tried to imagine his answer, I realized that no matter what he said, I would still want him to give me my baby back. The sadness of losing my child wouldn't suddenly go away just because God explained himself to me. If Jesus told me exactly why my baby had to die, I'd still want to die myself. And mysteriously, that gave me some sort of other answer. The answer was that I had to grieve. I had to acknowledge all the hurt and loss I was feeling. And eventually, I had to say goodbye.

So, I started talking to my friends more, about all that was going on inside my head. My friend Maureen said she'd written goodbye letters to the babies that she'd lost. She put them inside a helium balloon and released them in a park near her house. My friend Hillary told me not to be afraid to try and get pregnant again. She was a nurse and she said sometimes you're most fertile right after you miscarry. Ron told John to make sure I kept writing, and talking to him, about ALL my feelings.

But it was ultimately Sam who kept me going every day. He made me get out of bed even when I didn't want to. He was only two and a half, but he was more stubborn than me. He still needed to be taken care of, and he wouldn't take no for an answer. I grieved when I could, but there wasn't a lot of time to wallow. Plus, there was a ton of work to be done to get us all packed up and moved into the new townhouse we'd just bought. I had a tiny bit of hope that moving and settling into a new place would lead to a new pregnancy, which might be the stronger bit of hope needed to pull me out of my darkness for good.

One night, John was working late, and Sam was already in bed asleep, so I was all alone. I took a break from packing and put on a new CD. I stood in the living room staring down at our dark green corduroy couch and traced the raised vertical lines with my fingertips as David Crowder sang to me from our black and grey Aiwa stereo.

His song asked eight questions in a row, and I didn't have an answer for any of them. But I enjoyed the rhythm of their words so much that I absentmindedly tapped each syllable with my fingers and thumb. The questions reminded me of French class in high school, when we learned the difference between inversion and rising intonation, and we practiced our sentences aloud so we could figure out the right place to put the emphasis. The song was on repeat, and on the third time through, I realized I was deaf. I was the one who was blind. Technically, I could still hear and see, but because of my grief, the sounds I heard blurred into indistinguishable noise. Because of my broken heart, all the colors of the world glared into a single shade of grey.

It had been nearly two months since my failed pregnancy and I still felt broken and stuck. I'd thought it was all about the baby, but the day before I'd found myself telling Ron different stories about my Mom and Dad and even my little brother. It seemed like all the sad memories I'd previously anchored, came bobbing up to the surface on the heels of my new grief. I couldn't find any happy thoughts anywhere, and it made me wonder if I'd ever be able to feel happiness again.

In the background, David was singing about resurrection. I prayed along with the words I heard, but only barely. I was too tired to sing, too worn out to speak but the words did rise up from somewhere inside me. I still didn't know the answers to the questions David asked in his song, but I began to believe again that the answer to the questions Ron had asked me might just be yes.

Two weeks later, I was in my new house, peeing on another stick, and I dared to hope for a positive sign once again. I sat on new my bathroom floor and prayed that God wouldn't let the miscarriage be my last pregnancy. I sang quietly as I waited, and God gave us another gift. I spent the first five months praying for a little girl, and I still had so many questions: Why did you take that first baby, only to give me another one? Why couldn't we have skipped the miscarriage and just gone to a healthy pregnancy? What will happen if I lose another baby?

I spent the entire pregnancy waiting. Waiting for the baby, waiting for something to go wrong, waiting to go to the bathroom again, and scared every time I sat down on the toilet that I would see red again. Then it would be over, just like it was before.

Somehow delivery day came, and Laney was born on January 7, 2003. She was the best, easiest baby ever. Delivery was a breeze. She nursed and slept like a pro and she rarely cried. When my little princess turned one year old, I decided I'd just lived the fastest year of my life. Maybe because I subconsciously compared it to the year before she came, when every day, nearly every hour, was spent hoping and crying and waiting.

Later that Fall I decided to start a blog, after reading a couple of posts from some old college friends I'd found online. I wrote two stories about my friends in middle school, then one night I sat down and tried to tell this story. I cried the whole time I was writing the first page and had to quit in the middle of paragraph six. I didn't know how to end the story I wanted to share with people; I was afraid to finish it. I didn't want to risk being so vulnerable in front of the whole cyber universe. It had been eighteen months, and I didn't want whoever read my story to pity me. I wanted to write from a place of wholeness, to be able to tell my story with a happy ending, but I just wasn't there yet.

Several months passed and I found myself preparing for the Easter holiday by watching the newly released Passion of the Christ. There was a scene in the movie right after Jesus' death that spoke volumes to me. Mary was cradling the head of Jesus in her lap as she wept over his dead body. I saw how much she needed to see her baby boy again, even though he was already gone. She needed to hang onto him, to hug and kiss him, one last time, before she could let him go.

That's when I realized something major had been missing from my grieving process. It was the lack of anything physical. That's the thing I never had: tangible evidence of a loss. Menstrual cramping was the closest I got, and it felt exactly like every other period I'd ever had. I needed something I could look at, something I could touch and see to know that my baby was real; that my love for her was not imaginary.

So, I sat down to finish that initial blog post, hoping the complete story would bring me the physical closure I needed to move on. Strangely enough, as I started writing again, I remembered something that happened a few days after we lost the baby.

John and I had both contracted the pink eye at the same time, and we were both miserable. That night I took a long hot bath to help relieve the stress. My bleeding had slowed down enough that it no longer needed constant collection, so I let the water drain out as I lay there draining my own bottle of Dos Equis. When I finally sat up, my hand brushed against a small piece of something on the bottom of the tub. It was very tiny, like a small hangnail, and somewhat firm. At first, I thought it was a piece of candle wax, but when I tried to bend it, it wouldn't snap in two. I put it in my mouth and moved it around with my tongue. I pressed down on it gently with my teeth and it felt a bit spongy. Suddenly, I knew it was some kind of body tissue. I took it out of my mouth and stared at it again. I wondered if I could take it to a lab and have it examined; I felt like I needed the evidence. This was part of my dead child—I just knew it. I raked the entire length of the empty tub with my fingertips until I found two more pieces that were similar, and I gathered them up and placed them together gently on the side of the tub.

When I got out of the bath, I searched for a safe place to put them. I thought perhaps I should bury the pieces, but I didn't know how. Finally, I decided I needed to keep them for myself as some sort of proof. I wanted to watch and see if these pieces of flesh would decay, so I found a small, brown, oval jewelry case that snapped together with a gold clasp. I laid the pieces on top of an old Sacajawea coin and placed it carefully inside the case, then snapped it shut. Every so often those first few weeks, I took the case off my dresser and opened it, took out the pieces and held them and looked at them closely again. Then one day I opened the case a little too carelessly and the brassy coin fell out. All three pieces were lost in the faded fiber of my bedroom carpet. I never found them again.

"Grief must be witnessed to be healed," wrote Elizabeth Kubler Ross in her important book, *On Death and Dying*, so I wrote out all my grief and shared it with the world of the internet. My readers were my witnesses, standing beside me at the invisible grave of the daughter I never got to meet.

For I couldn't go on to be the Mom, wife, and writer that I wanted to be without paying tribute to her little life, no matter how short it was. She lived for almost six weeks, and I loved her for the last three days of her life. At twenty-five years old, losing her was the hardest thing I'd ever been through. And maybe I'm wrong, maybe the child was a boy. But I still believe what I did when I first started this essay. I believe my child is in heaven. I believe Jesus is stronger than death, and I believe I'll see her in heaven one day, if I ever get there. So, that's what I decided to name her that night: Paradise.

Sorry it took so long, sweetie.

Oyster Bay Harbour

2005

There's a song that came out the year Laney was born called "Blessed Be Your Name." We sang it at church a lot back then, back when my friend Valerie led the worship team, and had invited me to be part of it. I loved it at first, it's an upbeat tune that got a lot of radio play in the early 2000s. But in 2005, I found I couldn't sing it anymore. That's the year we lost baby number two, and I nearly lost my mind. It was not a time when "streams of abundance" were flowing, rather it felt more like walking a road "marked with suffering."

In January and February of that year we were trying to get pregnant. In March I found out we were, and by April, my belly was starting to stick out. But on the nineteenth of May I went to see the doctor and he couldn't find a heartbeat. Suddenly our baby was gone.

Somehow I made it to the parking garage after calling John, and the first thing I did after starting the car was turn the radio off. The breezy pop music I'd been listening to an hour before no longer matched the stifling heat of my empty car. Now I needed silence. I needed stillness. I wanted the world to stop spinning. I didn't listen to any music for several weeks afterward. Somehow it made everything hurt more. When I got to where I could listen again, mad songs were all I could tolerate. Eventually sad songs were acceptable. But singing worship music at church seemed like it would never be possible again.

During one of our conversations early on, John pointed out that the baby had lived for three months, so it made sense that we could grieve for at least three months. I went with the "least" part and set a goal for myself: I would feel better by the end of August. But grief is never that simple.

Regardless of what you've seen on TV, grief is more than just an hour of solemn tears at a funeral, or a black armband worn to work for a month. It's way more than a rainy afternoon at a graveyard or a pastel sympathy card in your mailbox. Grief can be messy and loud, but it can also be calculating, vindictive, and silent. It scares us so much that we either try to ignore it or we let it dictate our every action, but either extreme is dangerous. Pop psychology has taught us that it's good to be proactive when processing grief, but we're also terrified of letting it take over completely, knowing it has the potential to drown us. Which is why we tend to run from it, why we don't like to talk about it. Why we try to classify, formulate, and develop rules or stages for walking through it. We think that if we just know the steps, then we can take each one in a nice linear fashion and come out on the other side with just a minor wrinkle and a few more grey hairs.

Yet we can all name people who were never the same once they'd experienced great loss, and that scares us even more. The thought that we could become homeless alcoholics, or raging lunatics, or sad, strange cat lovers makes us hold back our tears and stiffen our upper lips, sucking in every sad sigh that threatens to escape our mouths.

Isn't it hard to believe some people used to know how long it was before you could wear a color other than black after a family member had died? Isn't it difficult to imagine living in a close-knit society that follows a strict set of rules regarding grief? Can you picture grieving people avoiding certain places or refusing to indulge in various activities, until their time of grieving is over? Can you see your neighbor, shaking his head at you if you dared to break one of these rules? No, of course not. You'd tell him to mind his own business, wouldn't you?

Because these days we've perfected the art of keeping our true feelings to ourselves. In our modern-day suburban fortresses, we lower the garage door drawbridge, drive across our driveway motes, and close up the castle's front doors. Communal life has become a thing of the past.

But once upon a time there were certain codes of behavior, developed in communities who faced grief after grief on a regular basis. Back when disease and illness were commonplace, and people lacked adequate shelter from the natural threats we don't think twice about anymore. But now we run the opposite risk. We have so much control over our lives, and everyday living has become so easy and pleasant, that we prefer to pretend there's no such thing as grief. And the result is our current mental health climate, which I gotta say, is pretty dreary.

Is there any way to return to the old ways of routine confession and small-town accountability? If we'd grown up in a different age, would we still struggle with grief all by ourselves, or would we have found other ways to express the sense of loss we often face in life?

I knew from my first experience with miscarriage that I couldn't escape grief, but all the things I did to try and honor this baby only made me more sad, and by the end of that summer I found myself in a very scary place.

After writing a letter, naming the baby, and having a makeshift funeral with John and our two remaining children, I didn't know what else to do but cry. And I cried a lot. At church services when people sang, at the zoo when we took our kids to visit John's family, in the upstairs bathroom when my milk came in. The physical reminders of my missing baby were everywhere, and I got so tired of facing them that I began to withdraw. I don't think it was a conscious decision, but somehow I turned my feelings off for a while, which turned out to be quite dangerous. I ended up caring for nothing and no one, not even myself. I was tempted to do things I knew I'd regret, bad things, just so I could feel something new. I even flirted with disaster, but thankfully couldn't follow through with it.

One night, in order to give me a little break, John took Sam and Laney out for dinner. But the quiet house was too quiet now, and I couldn't stand to feel so alone, so I put on my tennis shoes and headed out the door for a walk. We lived in a townhouse community at the time, with an open field and a large playground in the middle, where neighborhood roads jutted out like spokes on a wheel. As I reached the end of our street, I could see that the playground was empty, and decided to sprint to the slide. I ran as fast as I could, but I only made it a hundred yards before I began to cry. Crying made it harder to run and even harder to breathe, but I couldn't stop until I reached the slide, where I climbed the stairs and laid on my back. I stared up at a grey-white sky as hot tears slid from the corners of my eyes down to my hairline.

"Where are you, now?" I yelled out to the muggy air around me. I opened my eyes as wide as they would go, searching everywhere for a bit of warm color. I listened as hard as I could, begging for whispered assurance to blow across my skin. Then I raised my empty hands to the sky and pleaded to sense God's presence, but there was no hand reaching back for me this time, no glowing orb of heavenly light. There was simply nothing, and nothingness took over for a while.

At the beginning of August, I started going to therapy again, and saying everything out loud, to an objective, listening ear helped, but it wasn't enough. I started having trouble with everyday tasks. Cooking dinner and shopping for groceries overwhelmed me. I'd head out to Target and end up at Walmart because I couldn't remember which was where. I lay in bed at night exhausted, yet unable to sleep. My therapist told me she thought I was in a double depression. She said it sounded like I suffered from dysthymia, or chronic mild depression, which meant that my "normal" mood was often pretty low, and my inner psyche didn't think it was worth it to try and return to that state.

That might sound like psychological mumbo-jumbo to you, but for me it was something new to hold onto, as I began to understand and have a name for my illness. It was very freeing to give myself permission to have sadness that was beyond my control, and not just the result of bad circumstances or weak faith, so in September I made the important decision to go see my doctor and ask her to prescribe an antidepressant for me.

Soon after that I decided to get the tattoo I'd been contemplating for four years. After our first miscarriage, I'd considered it for a while, but all I could think to have done were initials–and I barely had the guts to walk into a tattoo shop–let alone answer any questions about my ink. I didn't want to be on the receiving end of weird looks, and I certainly didn't want to have to make small talk about tattoos with well-meaning strangers in the grocery line.

What I'd really wanted was some remembrance, but I didn't have a graveside to visit, or even a picture from an ultrasound. I'd longed for a tangible witness to that suffering, but my creative sparks were doused by fear and I ended up doing nothing.

Four years later, I was older, perhaps a bit wiser—probably not any less fearful— but way more resolute. There would be no more hiding out, no more trying to move on, no more getting back to normal life. What was normal life anyway? I sure didn't know. My heart was broken, shredded to pieces, and ground into the dirt. How could I look at life the same way again, after being anesthetized, intubated, and dilated, all with no delivery? After my lifeless child had been sucked from my womb and deposited in a place only doctors knew of, there was no way "normal life" was even an option.

The day I got my tattoo was kind of exciting, as exciting as it can be to let a stranger use a needle to bury ink beneath your skin. The result wasn't much larger than the small card you might attach to a Christmas present, located to the right of my navel, just above the hip bone. It's a picture of two flowers, freshly picked, and resting in an imaginary vase. The pink daisy is smaller and slightly turned away, as if blown by the wind. It represents Emmaline Paradise, the first baby we lost. The blue one is bigger and faces forward, it's for Jacob Andrew.

As soon as I saw it, I smiled, I felt really, really good—and no, I hadn't started my medication yet. That happened the next day. But the ink was my spoon-full of sugar. It was exactly what I needed to help the medicine go down. Even though I'd said goodbye and done the best I could to mourn. Even though we'd held a memorial and set our little sailor out to sea, I needed more, more than our fetus obsessed culture had offered me. I needed to plant flowers in the cemetery, to bring a little beauty from all those ashes.

In my fight to find emotional health, this tattoo serves as a monument. It marks the beginning of a long and bitter battle. I don't know when it will ever be over, but the day I got pricked, I turned the tide. I gained the upper hand. I fought back and declared that I would not be taken out. I think my baby was proud of me that day. When the pain reached its worst, I shed a few tears. They were more for baby Jake than for the needle. I couldn't verbalize it then, but as I write it occurs to me, and maybe you can relate. Isn't it strange? Isn't it funny–how a huge, ugly, old wound can begin to heal through another one– one that's small, pretty and new?

In October, I started going back to practice with the praise band at church, but I still couldn't sing a song that declared, "You give and take away," without sobbing. And as I tore another page off the calendar to see where it said "Baby Due" on November second, the tears still came.

The "give and take" line comes from Job, chapter one, verse twenty-one. It says that Job fell to the ground in worship, saying, "Naked I came from my mother's womb, and naked I will depart. The Lord gave and the Lord has taken away; may the name of the Lord be praised." But I think it's probably that he couldn't stand, rather than feeling particularly reverent at that moment. And don't forget that this was after he shaved his head (not an easy task in the time before electric, or hand-held, razors) and tore his robe to pieces. Later in the story, Job shouts, he tells his friends off, and he wishes God had never made him. And it's okay for him to do all these things, to feel all these feelings. God says he never sinned. Worship means your heart bowed down to God, and your life reflects it even when you're not raising your hands and saying, "Hallelujah!"

Because how can you celebrate life if you're not willing to mourn the loss of it? It's like a mathematical equation or two scales that are equally balanced. If having is wonderful, then not having is awful. It has to be. It has to be terrible so the opposite can be magical.

More magic came to us in the Summer of 2006, when we found out we were pregnant again, with Benjamin Bailey, born on March 9, 2007. My pregnancy with Ben was completely normal in the physical sense, but rather anxious in the emotional one, and as soon as he arrived, I knew I never wanted to risk getting pregnant again. The only other birth I was concerned about after Ben came along was the birth of my writing career. That gestation took way more than nine months, but the life that's come out of it (not the published books, mind you) just keeps on getting richer. I can't wait to tell you about it.

High Forest Lane

2006

I don't know if every writer has days like this or if it's just me. I don't know if it's a severe lack of self-esteem, chronic depression, a spiritual battle, or just Monday. What I do know is that today, I don't like myself at all. And I'm not just talking about superficial stuff, like wishing I were taller and thinner. I mean that right now, it feels like I'm a worthless human being with nothing important to say. I don't feel like I'm a good enough friend or a loving enough wife, and I'm pretty sure I'm a lazy daughter, too. I can't even consider how I'm doing as a mother today, because it feels like there's no possible way I'm currently in charge of three other humans.

I wish I were lying or being dramatic. There's nothing too difficult going on right now. We have good jobs, stability, and the ability to pay our bills and buy most of what we need. Nothing is broken and no one is ill. I feel a little tired, but it doesn't seem to be any more than usual, and I wasn't feeling like this at all until a couple of hours ago. In fact, this morning, I woke up in a good mood. I knew I had most of the day to myself, so I did the things I normally do on writing days. After I took the kids to school, I made myself a nice breakfast, poured a cup of tea, and sat down to eat. Then I prayed and read some chapters in Psalms. My plan after that was to get to work.

My usual goal is to write for two hours, at least three days a week. But I didn't sit right down and get to work today because I was feeling scared, tempted to believe the final product wouldn't be worth the process I had to go through to get it. When I get like that, it's extra hard to ignore everything else I typically do as a wife, mom, and part-time caregiver. So, naturally, I distracted myself by taking a shower. Then I got overwhelmed thinking about spending two whole hours with nothing but me and my brain, so I found other stuff to do for three more hours. Finally, I went out to lunch by myself, and stopped by the church office to visit with some friends. But after I'd been there about thirty minutes, everyone else needed to get back to work. By the time I got home, I only had an hour and a half left to get any writing done before picking up the kids from school.

When I finally sat down at my laptop an hour ago, I felt intimidated and weary, so I got out a pen and paper and scribbled down random thoughts and feelings on a blank sheet of paper for fifteen minutes. I forced myself to string words together, but they didn't make much sense, so I began to cry. Then I stopped writing and cried some more. Finally, it was time to get the kids, and I had to admit defeat for the day. Again.

The process of writing can be hard for a person who struggles with low self-esteem and depressive tendencies. Sometimes it feels like I'm looking at a gaping hole in my leg, knowing there's no doctor around to help me stitch it up. I know I have to do it. I know it's gonna hurt, and I know I'm gonna cry, so it's much easier to keep pretending the wound doesn't exist.

But it does. And I'm determined not to ignore it anymore. Writing is a major step on the road to healing for me, and wholeness is something I know I'm supposed to seek. It's one of the things I was made for. It doesn't matter if no one else ever sees my work. It doesn't matter if it stinks when I'm finished. (Okay, that one doesn't feel true yet.) What matters, what really matters most of all, is that I keep on trying ... Right?

The hardest thing about writing this particular chapter is knowing what I want it to be about, which is how I learned to love my life enough to write all these words about it. But it's kind of like a hypochondriac deciding to read a medical journal. There's no way of looking in this mirror and not seeing my own wrinkles. And I have a lot of wrinkles.

But that's just it. I'm not a therapist. I'm not a professor. My one and only degree is in English Education. I'm not (technically) qualified to talk about any of this. All I have is my own experience. But it's the most reliable research I have access to, so here goes.

Before Ben came along, we decided to move again. John had been looking for jobs that would take us back to Arkansas for a couple of years, but nothing ever came along. So, two years after his parents relocated to Knoxville, we decided to follow them. Just before the housing bubble burst in 2007, we were able to sell our townhouse for twice what we bought it for, paying off all our debt with enough left to live on 'til we found jobs in Tennessee. So, we packed up our newly purchased Scion, with our two kids and one cat in tow, and drove the ten hours to John's parents' house in Farragut, where we ended up living for the next six months.

While we were living in their basement the one-year anniversary of losing baby Jake loomed large and I decided to mark its passing with a series of posts on my blog. My original idea was based on the fact that I was learning what it meant to have a sense of grief, and because I dabble in puns, I decided to write a post a day for the entire week–each one corresponding to one of the five senses. The anniversary was on a Friday, but I only posted Monday through Wednesday. Turns out that the senses of taste and smell do not easily lend themselves to meaningful metaphors regarding life and death, or maybe they do and I just didn't know how to write about them yet, but by the end of the week I didn't much care. I'd done all the grief work I could muster for that first anniversary, while still being able to care for two small children.

Sam was in second grade by then, and Laney was going to Mother's Day Out a couple of days a week, so that's when I stayed home to write. But that was before summer came and I decided to take on a part time job as the pastor's assistant at our new church. The month after that we moved into our new house, and two months later we found out I was pregnant with Ben.

Those anniversary posts were the first ones that managed to go beyond the small circle of family and friends I had made on the internet. For the first time I started receiving emails and comments from total strangers who found comfort in my words. That's when I knew I wanted writing to become more than a hobby. I had no idea what kind of books I might try to publish some day, but I knew I had stories to tell. I never imagined I would write so much poetry either, but my love for rhythm and rhyme and creating memorable scenes became a hunger that wouldn't keep quiet anymore. Even when I doubted my ability to share anything coherent with the world, poems kept showing up, to help me sort out the feelings and mysteries I couldn't explain in essay form.

For several months I tried to build an audience and hone my craft, but after Ben arrived, writing days became sporadic at best, and non-existent the rest of the time. I spent many days in frustration, wishing my kids were older, wishing I could go back to college and retake all the writing classes I skipped the first time I was in school, wishing I knew more artists who could show me the ropes, and guide me on the road toward the writing life.

Thankfully, when Ben was about eighteen months old, Andrew Peterson came to town for a concert and John and I went with some friends to see the show. Andrew and his brother Pete had recently launched a new website called the Rabbit Room which John and I had been following for a couple of months. After the show we got in line to shake AP's hand and I handed him a note I'd written earlier that day suggesting that the site needed more female contributors. The note got stuck in the bottom of Andrew's backpack for six months, but one sunny day in May, I got an email from him saying he'd visited my site and would love it if I submitted something to the Rabbit Room for publication. Two years later we helped the Peterson brothers pull off the first Hutchmoot, and we became part of a community that's influenced my creative life ever since. From helping me find and foster a local writer's group here in Knoxville, to inspiring me to write this book, to teaching me how to find my own voice and giving me the chance to use it, the Rabbit Room/Hutchmoot community has been an invaluable resource.

There have been many tough writing days since I began pursuing my dreams in earnest, a lot like the one I described at the beginning of this essay. But every now and then I wake up with a new idea and actually have the time and space necessary to plant that seed and nurture it 'til it blooms. And the resulting flowers have been sustenance for my soul.

But if you really want to grow as an artist, it helps to have stability. Being in one house for more than ten years can do that for a person, even if her kids are providing constant change. In fact, the large gap of years that passed between this chapter and the next are the years I spent growing this book, as well as my three kids. And while it makes for an awkward timeline, I'm so thankful for the sense of place and belonging that came to me through those years. For time is often the most important element in art making. And like a child who walks the same path every day, the attentive artist eventually learns to stop tripping over the same stones.

One Spring I went to a Women's Retreat at an old Catholic church in Sewanee, Tennessee. I shared a room with a friend in St. Mary's dormitory, with a window that overlooked one of the most dramatic and beautiful valleys I've ever seen. We were perched near the edge of a cliff in the woods of a serene little town for four whole days. It should have been a dream weekend, but it wasn't, because I was in pain.

Five days before the retreat I had fallen and bruised my tailbone while roller skating, and there was virtually no position, other than standing, that felt comfortable. Which would have been fine if I was on a four-day walk-about by myself, but I was on a four day sit-about with a hundred other women. Most of the time, we sat in a conference room and listened to speakers, and when we weren't sitting to listen, we were sitting to eat and to visit with other women. It was a very uncomfortable experience, but the fact that everyone around me could tell how miserable I was made me even more uncomfortable. I don't like to be the center of attention when I'm feeling confident and energetic, let alone when I'm needy and in pain. I tried to fade into the background, which didn't really work as I was constantly carrying around a large donut shaped cushion.

I was with a group of church ladies after all, and there's nothing we like better than taking care of someone else. There was no way to escape the barrage of sympathetic questions: "How are you feeling today? Is your tailbone still hurting? Would you like to try sitting in this chair instead?" On and on the attention was poured, and the more I brushed it aside, the more intense it became. I stood out like a bear cub at a picnic table.

To make matters worse, this was the kind of retreat where I was supposed to focus on myself. That's what my friend Susan told us when she began the first session on Thursday night. "Thank you for taking the risk to answer this invitation, Ladies," she said. "Jesus wants to meet with you, here, over these next few days." Susan looked at us all in earnest before continuing. "This time is worth all the trouble you took to make it happen," she assured us. "You are worth it."

The problem was I couldn't believe her. Not one little bit. Oh, I wanted to of course, but all I could think about was my sore bottom. The theme for the weekend was culled from a few verses in Ephesians chapter 3 that talk about "being rooted and established in love," and having "power ... to grasp how wide and long and high and deep is the love of Christ." It was a message I found difficult to receive as I sat awkwardly upon my blue donut pillow, listening to speaker after speaker.

One afternoon during a covenant of silence I walked around the grounds and found an old wooden bench that was curved just so, that when I sat down, for the first time in days, nothing hurt. In that instant the Holy Spirit seemed to hover in the air beside me saying, "See? I do care about your pain." I was tempted to brush it aside like I had all the ladies who'd offered me their attention over the weekend, but as I wrote out a prayer I found myself wondering whether my pain really was important to God, and not just the physical pain I was in that weekend either. What if all the pain of life, including the emotional baggage I carried around in my little ragamuffin heart had some ultimate purpose? What if God wanted to use it to help me find my true self, one that was strong and full of joy? What if he wanted to redeem it somehow? So, I could share my painful stories with others and help them find meaning in their pain.

I wish I could say I came home from that weekend renewed and ready to finish my book, but no, there were a few more bumps and bruises still to come.

I'd been working on this book for a few years by then but had lately become consumed with figuring out the kind of writer I wanted to be, and before I knew it, I'd overwhelmed myself with comparison to other writers. The result was debilitating shame. And fear. I was tempted to parse each sentence I wrote, finding all the flaws before I ever pressed the period key. I got so caught up in trying to write better, that I stopped writing at all, for over a year. It was ridiculous, like thinking I couldn't run anymore just because I couldn't go very fast or make it very far. But I still had two working legs. They could still get me from one place to another. I just needed to start using them again.

But it took some preparatory action on my part. First, I made sure to get a few nights of really good sleep, which meant I had to kick my snoring husband out to the couch. Then I made an appointment with my doctor and spoke honestly about how rough my moods had been. He put me back on an antidepressant, even though I'd been off it for five years. I also started taking some vitamin supplements and getting a little bit of exercise—often just a fifteen-minute walk—a couple of times a week. Slowly, I started feeling better. And once I started feeling better, I was able to believe the truth enough to start writing again.

And what was that truth you ask? It's the truth of the gospel, that I belong to my Abba, Father. The one who cares about every detail of my life, including the painful parts. He's seen me perching awkwardly on the sidelines of my own life, again and again over the years, and each time he longs to give me the medicine necessary to help me get back in the game, and maybe even score. Whether that's actual medication, or healing old grief wounds and correcting false patterns of thinking, Christ has the tools to make me well. He's equipped some wonderful saints who truly know what it means to bear one another's burdens, and those pastors, friends, and therapists have helped me find life again. I pray the same will happen for you, if you find yourself relating a little too well to some of these stories of mine.

I can't say who else is meant to be a writer like me, and I don't know that therapy and medication are always necessary for healing, but I believe everyone has beauty in their hearts that's meant to be shared with the world. And I further believe it's their job to look for that beauty, even if it takes years and years to find it. Even if they have to dig through a whole lot of shit to figure out where it's hiding. Because there's more to being healed than simply "not hurting anymore." No matter what kind of death is endured, there's always new life to be found. Isn't that the ultimate lesson of the resurrection? And shouldn't the lives of Christ's followers reflect that power?

Perhaps that's too preachy for a memoir, but it's what I've come to believe after writing nearly fifty-thousand words about my life. My friend Carrie taught me that lament is always directional, and after ten years of choosing to direct my lamentations toward God, perhaps I'm beginning to understand how he wants things to work. But don't worry, I've still got a whole lot left to figure out.

Kerry Way

2015

In November I shared a poem on my blog that admitted I'd been struggling with thoughts of suicide that month. The words for the poem came pouring out of me that Friday morning, after I read some psalms and tried to pray. My kids were at school and John was at the gym while I sat crying in a recliner by the window. I'd had many sad mornings that Fall but things were actually starting to look brighter when I shared the poem, otherwise I'd never have been able to write, or post it.

Before the sad mornings started, I was mad, like all the time. I feel sorry for my family members and the kids who were in my preschool class back then. I lost my temper at least three times a day. I'd snap at people for minor infractions and yell at them for bigger ones. Other times I'd hit a wall, or kick at one of our pets. Once I got mad enough to have a good cry I felt better, but most of the time I settled for being pissy-just angry enough to remain completely miserable.

By the end of October, the anger began to turn into sadness and lethargy. I signed up for an exercise class to try and boost my mood and energy, but by the end of class I was spent, so depleted I couldn't stay for the cool down. The few times I tried, a deep sorrow welled up in me, and by the time I got to my car, I was weeping. I've been known to get a little teary when I'm completely relaxed, but this was more intense than that. Something was wrong, and I knew it. I tried to talk myself out of it for a couple of weeks, waiting to bounce back from my "bad mood," but nothing changed, and I soon lost the motivation to fight it off.

One day John came home and found me crying and I couldn't explain why. He sat with me at our kitchen table as I covered my face with my hands and sobbed. He listened as I told him that I had no reason to feel so sad. "It's not logical," I said. "I know that–I keep telling myself that–but I can't figure out how to turn it off."

John hugged me while I cried, and although I was thankful for his comfort, I felt really embarrassed. When he went back to work, he sent me a text with a quote from a book he'd been reading called *The Book of the Dun Cow*. It was the perfect response from someone in his position, someone who's never suffered this kind of episode. Here's what it said:

"He went wordless, and wordless he sat beside her. He knew the size of her sorrow."

It was a few more days before I called my doctor. It was so hard to work up the courage to tell a total stranger that I needed help. I got so desperate that I texted a friend and asked her to do it for me. She probably would have, too, but she was taking care of small children and didn't see the text until several hours later. I remember lying in bed with my phone in my hand, feeling crushed by shame. It took all the strength I had to push against that weight and dial the number, but I knew I had to do it. There was no other way for me to get free.

* * *

On the morning of February eleventh, 2014, I received one of the worst phone calls of my life. It was nine-thirty and I was sitting at my desk at work. My boss was in a meeting and the other two women I worked with were nestled quietly in their cubicles across the aisle from me. Our elderly clients typically called the financial firm early in the morning, but things had been quiet so far that day. The new secretary hadn't started yet, so I was first in line to answer the phone when it rang. When I picked up, I looked at the caller ID and saw that it was my husband calling, but he didn't say anything when I first said "Hello."

"What?" I finally asked the silence at the other end.

"Um, I don't know how to say this..." he trailed off. I could tell by his soft tone that something bad had happened, I just couldn't tell how bad.

"Just tell me," I demanded, starting to panic.

"Well, I just got off the phone with Tim Tucker," he paused again. "Apparently ... Carter shot himself this morning."

I nearly dropped the phone in shock. I don't remember what I said next. I don't know what else John said either. I remember swallowing lots of air and gripping the Formica countertop with my fingertips. After a minute or so my co-workers could tell something was wrong and they both began walking over toward my desk. Eventually I hung up the phone and whispered the awful news back to them.

Tim was an elder at our church, and Carter was the best friend of his son Seth. Seth was the best friend of our son, Sam. The three boys attended a private Christian school together, and Carter was only fifteen.

John told me he was on his way to Sam's school so he could pick him up and bring him home. I left work to go and meet them there. One of my co-workers offered to drive me but I told her I felt like I needed to be alone. We were all shaky and tearful, but I knew that I was still holding back a great deal of emotion.

Once I got in the van, it felt safer to let go and really cry. After a couple of miles, my tears turned into prayers. After several more minutes, the prayers became audible.

"Where were you?" I yelled past the steering column.

"How could you let this happen?" I demanded of the cold car window.

"This just isn't right!" I shouted up at the empty grey sky.

"This is so wrong I can't even think about it right now!"

On and on, the whole fifteen minutes home, I railed at God. I screamed. I cussed. I cried. I told him he'd really messed up on this one. At one point it seemed as though a faint image of Christ were standing out on the road in front of me and I felt the urge to mash my gas pedal to the floor and await the unavoidable impact, but some angel force reached down and kept me steady. It was the most physical "spiritual" sensation I'd ever felt, and it scared me just as much as if I'd seen Moses' burning bush. Maybe that sounds like God was upset with me for losing my temper, but that's not at all how it felt. Instead I sensed that he was raging along with me. As if I could see beyond the veil, into the spiritual realm for just a millisecond, and I knew there was more than I could comprehend going on, so all I could do was surrender and weep.

I made it back to the house a few minutes before Sam and John. I stood in my silent kitchen and tried to remember how to breathe.

When they got there, I hugged Sam like I've never hugged him before. For a whole week I couldn't let him out of my sight for more than five minutes. I was scared to let him sleep alone downstairs. I took all the karate belts and belts for his pants out of his room, and made sure our one rifle was not loaded, that the bullets were locked up tight. I bought him whatever kind of junk food he wanted and let him watch whatever TV shows he wanted. For months I made sure to never leave him by himself for too long, and I over-analyzed every single word that came out of his mouth.

But Sam never wanted to talk about any of it. He wrote a sweet post on Carter's Facebook page that afternoon and that was the end of it. For him. On the surface anyway. As a borderline Asperger's kid, Sam had rarely been emotionally attached to anyone outside our immediate family. Plus, he was a teenager, and a guy. He was not about to sit down and pour out his heart to me about all that he was feeling.

For several days afterward, Sam was more clingy and affectionate than usual. The night after it happened, we snuggled up on my bed to watch a new Sherlock Holmes show together. Sam fell asleep halfway through the episode and I spent the next forty-five minutes counting his breaths.

Then it snowed for three days. Schools closed and traffic stopped. It felt like the whole town was grieving. Finally, we got up on Saturday morning and put on our dress clothes and went to the funeral. I was tearful the entire time we were there, vacillating between anger and sorrow. I nearly walked out when the worship leader asked us to put aside our sadness and praise Jesus. I knew I couldn't make this about me though, so I kept my arm around Sam and he put his head on my shoulder from time to time, but I never saw any tears in his eyes.

Sometime over the next week all the guys from Sam and Seth's small group got together to play video games at Seth's house and I remember how Sam felt like it was important for him to be there for Seth. He knew Seth's friendship with Carter predated Sam's friendship with him, so he wanted the focus of this loss to be on Seth. That day, when I drove Sam over to Seth's house, he pulled up a Beatles' song to play from his iPhone in the car. Paul's voice was clear and soothing coming from the small speaker, giving us both a peaceful phrase for the afternoon, "Let it be."

I count it as both a blessing and a difficulty that I never really knew Carter. Sure, I'd seen him in the pick-up line at school many times, and Sam had replayed several of their school day conversations for us at the dinner table the past couple of years. They often sat together with a few other boys at lunch, but Carter never came over to our house and Sam never hung out with him outside of school. I knew Carter had a crush on a girl at their school and had recently asked her to go to homecoming with him. I also knew that he and Sam had had many conversations about superhero movies and their mutual appreciation for classical music, as well as possibly transferring to public school next year.

But that's it; that's all that I can remember. I never met his family before the day of the funeral, and I haven't seen or talked with them since. Carter didn't leave behind a note, so all anyone could do was speculate why he'd done what he'd done. Everyone said he was a quiet kid, but no one ever suspected that he was depressed, at least not enough to end his own life. His church, family, and school communities were all shocked by his suicide.

When I was a sophomore in college, I became obsessed with a song by Annie Lennox called "Why?" So, obsessed that I created a dance routine while listening to it, which was always alone, in my dorm room, with my eyes closed. But I'm not a dancer. The only dance class I ever attended was *Intro to Ballet*–which I also took when I was a sophomore–and I didn't learn enough to go around making up choreography for random music I heard on the radio. I'd also never thought of doing that for any other song ever, and haven't since. So, what made me do it for this song? What was it about those lyrics that haunted me so? Why did I thrive on that particular melodious melancholy for six whole months?

Why?

Exactly. Go listen to the song. You'll see what I'm talking about.

One Friday morning, just before Christmas break, I went to see the guidance counselor on campus. His name was Keldon Henley. Of course it was. I mean, what else was he gonna grow up to be, with a name like that? I told Keldon, in confidence of course, that I thought I might be depressed, and he told me I was probably just dealing with what most people called the Sophomore Slump. His prescription was as follows:

1. *Go home and be with your family for the weekend.*
2. *Sleep late and be lazy. Watch your favorite cartoons on Saturday morning.*
3. *Eat cereal, or soup, maybe something like Cheerios, or whatever other comforting foods you can find to slurp from a bowl.*

I've never forgotten this advice. It was the strangest thing I'd ever heard, but it was practical enough that I did make use of it that weekend and I guess I bounced back alright the next semester. I don't remember following this prescription any other time, but it seems a good enough recipe for dealing with the Sophomore Slump. The question is, how do you know when you're dealing with something more serious than a slump, and what do you do then?

Singer songwriter David Wilcox tells a story about a friend who had an old car that started breaking down all the time, so one day the friend finally had to ask himself: Do I have a car, or just a hobby? That's kind of how I feel about Depression. I often have to ask myself: Is this just a dark cloud passing over, or am I stuck inside the midnight cave again? The key thing I look for is how long my bad mood lasts. If it's more than three days, I know it's time to look outside myself for help.

When I used to have a monthly cycle, my moods were easier to track. I often found myself in a funk right before my period started. In the middle of those funks, if I could remember to consult the calendar, I would see that yes, indeed, I should be getting my period in a day or two. And usually, after that initial rush of estrogen, I began feeling better. Looking at the date gave me permission to relax and feel whatever I was feeling–anger, sadness, some combination of both–knowing it would soon pass. When I know good days are still ahead of me, it's easier to hang on and ride the rough waves, but when you can't see the end of your funk, it's hard to believe that's all it is.

Kerri Way, 2015

Now that I've had a hysterectomy my cycle is less predictable, and I have to be more vigilant about watching my moods. Whenever I'm in a funk and can't immediately identify the reason behind it, I start to worry that Depression has come back. One of the scariest things about Depression is that once you're deep inside it, it can convince you that you feel the worst you've ever felt and you will never feel good again, no matter what you do. Medicine, counseling, skydiving, it all feels hopeless. So, for me, constant vigilance is the best way I know to stay ahead of the curve and make sure I don't end up relapsing.

The tricky thing for some of us is that Depression is more than just feeling sad and crying all the time, so sometimes it sneaks up on you. For me, it can start out looking like I'm irritable or extra sensitive, but I soon find myself hating everything about my life. I look in the mirror and see all my worst features, magnified by ten. I think about my relationships and wish for more, and better, relationships; then ultimately decide they all stink. I can't bring myself to try anything new because I'm sure I will fail. Everyday decisions like "what should I cook for dinner tonight?" become as overwhelming as walking a tightrope made of dental floss. Until doing the most normal things becomes impossible, because there are loud voices in my head telling me I suck at everything and no one really likes me.

Before I know it, the worst form of tunnel vision takes over. When I'm in that state, peripheral vision is non-existent. I home in on what's upsetting me, and no amount of outside interference can break my focus. "Stop thinking about that all the time," someone might say to me, and my immediate reaction is to stare harder. It's like an obsessive-compulsive disorder, or the opposite of ADD. It's all encompassing and it's utterly exhausting.

Depression can be temporary, brought on by a particular circumstance, and easily dissolved once the circumstance is resolved; but without treatment it often becomes a permanent way of thinking and viewing the world, like wearing yellow tinted lenses in your most comfortable pair of glasses. Some days I find myself wishing there was a mute button for the remote control of my world. Some days it feels like I have a sunburn, an ear infection, and night blindness–all at the same time. I don't want anyone to touch me, and I don't want to listen to music, or watch TV, and I certainly don't want to talk to anyone. I just want to be left alone, to sit outside in a hammock, in the middle of the woods, in eighty-five-degree weather–with nothing but a soft, blue sky to close my eyes against.

I often describe Depression to people who've never experienced it like this: Pretend you're a six-cylinder engine but only four of your cylinders are working properly. It's not just being tired or sad, although you often feel like you could sleep or cry for days. Yet other times you feel so tense you can't breathe properly, so you have to get outside and run, or jump up and down, or scream and pull your hair, just at the roots, until it hurts enough that you can't think about anything else. I've also been known to pinch my arm, or bite down on my thumb really hard. Anything that stops the mental drainpipe swirl and forces me to focus on a physical sensation for a while, until my brain catches up.

Not all those solutions are healthy, though. The healthiest thing I can do is call a friend and be vulnerable about how I'm feeling, but it's taken years of practice for me to learn how to do that. Once I'm honest about how my day is going, my friend can help me see if it's just a bad day or if I need to take a closer look at the overall status of my mental health, and maybe go see a doctor or counselor for a checkup. Because sometimes medication stops working, and other times it just needs a boost, like talk therapy, for a while.

* * *

Once I started taking an antidepressant again, I began sleeping better. I'd forgotten what deep sleep was like and how it felt to have a rested mind in the morning. Long term sleep deprivation has serious side effects, but most people don't notice because it happens so gradually. The next thing I noticed was that I became less irritable. I kept finding myself blowing out a sigh rather than clenching my jaw in rage. And it was so nice to be able to take that deep breath, to be able to think for a second, before immediately reacting to whatever stimulus was in front of me. It was so nice to not feel supreme annoyance at every little thing that didn't go my way, to begin seeing things I liked again, rather than obsessing about the things I didn't.

After several weeks I felt like the sadness was dissipating. I still cried a lot, but my tears began to feel more like a faucet that turned off and on, rather than a river I couldn't see the end of. I started smiling more and laughing louder and liking the person I saw when I looked in the mirror. I also felt less anxious about writing. Where before I had to clean my whole house, make a cup of tea, light a candle, and pray before I got started; now I could just sit down and start working. I wasn't as worried about getting every word right the first time. I knew that I could come back to it and make things better the second time. And I had plenty of time. There was no longer this insane pressure to become famous before everyone forgot about me. I could just do the writing I wanted to do, and tell the stories I want to tell. Whatever was supposed to happen with those stories would happen. Well, I didn't believe that all the time, but it was much easier than it used to be.

And that's the biggest change I see even now, the ability to see things in a different light. To know that this moment is not the only one there is. I can see more clearly all the moments that came before, and I trust more fully in all the moments yet to come. Because inside each one of those moments is an opportunity to be my best self, rather than a cancerous tumor of fear.

The root of this shift in perspective, I believe, is less shame about my feelings. Initially my medicine helped with that, but now what helps the most is talking with other people (counselors and friends) who have lots of big feelings like me. Shame is the killer weapon of depression, the thing that keeps us from telling anyone all the crazy things we're feeling, for fear they won't want to be our friends anymore. It makes our thoughts sound something like this:

If people really know how desperate I feel, they'll think it's all my fault. They'll tell me to stop being so narcissistic and pray more. They'll tell me about all the other people they know who have real problems, who don't go around whining about their feelings all the time. They'll tell me to just get over it, to cheer up, to move on, and a thousand other things that'll make me hate myself more than I already do.

Because that's what Depression really is, hating yourself.

On a really bad day last year I tried to read Psalm 139 out loud to myself, but I couldn't do it. The words would not come out of my mouth. Nothing came out but sobs, and the revelation that I didn't believe a single word on the page. This was not humility. It was self-hatred, and it was not from God. He did not want me to feel condemned, but I did, and no amount of prayer or truth could knock it out of me.

This is the kind of mental illness that makes people finally pull that shaky trigger, or walk out into the middle of the ocean, or cut off their own ears. It's a disease we don't fully understand, but it's a disease nonetheless, an arbiter of death, in all its forms. And we've got to start treating it that way. We've got to be able to talk about it, and encourage each other to get the help we need to fight it.

So here I am writing an entire chapter about it. If you're struggling with Depression, please tell someone. I know there are people who will say the wrong things, who don't truly understand, but that doesn't mean they don't care. Find someone you trust and be as honest as you can stand. Fumble through the awkward darkness until someone can help you find the light switch. Do not keep crying alone in your bleak corner. You are wonderfully made, in the image of a God who does not hate himself, who doesn't want you to hate yourself either. You have nothing to be ashamed of. Even if you don't believe it.

The things you think, feel, and believe when you're depressed are simply not true. No matter how much they feel like it. They are symptoms of an unwell mind, and the first step in treating those symptoms is not obsessing over what caused it. Whether it's a tendency you were born with, a chemical imbalance, a spiritual funk, or the stress of hard times in your life, the first step in treatment is opening up.

* * *

It was a hot summer day when I finally got up the nerve to go and visit Carter's grave. It sits in a small cemetery in the middle of the suburbs, next to a church called *The River of Living Waters*. Before I got out of the car, I read aloud Psalm 139, giving special attention to verse eight, where the Psalmist proclaims that even if he makes his bed in Sheol, God's holy spirit is with him. It comforted me even as it caused me grief to imagine Carter's final moments here on earth. I continued to cry as I walked to the far side of the graveyard, where I tucked a small seashell into a corner of the headstone. The day before I'd taken a Sharpie pen and written words from First Corinthians on the smooth pink surface inside the conch. "The last enemy to be destroyed is death," it said. Let it be, dear Lord. Let it be.

Kerri Way

2017

Last Fall I had a brand-new puppy in my lap and a broken heart in my chest. It was the beginning of the last year at home for my son Sam, and I bought the puppy because I needed something warm and soft to hold. It was the only thought that made me feel good during that first month back to school. For three weeks I'd laid on the couch crying every morning, and the only reason worth getting up that I could imagine was to go visit the pet store. But I hadn't acted quickly enough with the first two puppies I met, so when Rory caught my eye I didn't hesitate. I filled out the paperwork immediately and she came home with us two days later.

A week after we got Rory, Sam decided he didn't want to go to church anymore, because he didn't believe in God anymore, and my grief became more complicated. Not only did I have a son who would soon be leaving home for the first time, he seemed to be running away from us as well, as fast and as far as possible.

Around the middle of October, I started regretting my decision to get a puppy. Rory was six months old by then. She was sleeping through the night just fine, and had house trained really well; but her personality had blossomed into a boisterous, barky one, and she was driving everyone crazy.

It was November before I realized what I'd done–tried to replace a child with a dog. Getting a puppy was my attempt to fill the hole I knew would be left when Sam went away to college. I guess I thought I could just bypass the grief I knew was coming; but my solution had turned out to be a loud mess, who only amplified the emptiness in my aching heart.

I don't remember much about December except that I started getting stomach aches and couldn't eat anything but bowls of cereal. When I finally went to the doctor, they put me on Prilosec and upped my dose of antidepressant. By Christmas I was feeling better, but when we were getting ready to leave my family's house my sister hugged me and told me they'd see me again at Sam's graduation. I burst into tears. It was the first time I'd visualized that moment, and the reality that it would be happening in less than five months overwhelmed me.

If this makes me sound like a drama queen, so be it, but I've never been one of those moms who cry when their babies go back to school. I'm not the kind of woman who yells at the TV during football games, or makes a scene in a restaurant. I don't like to be the center of attention, and I'm super embarrassed when people make a big deal out of me. I don't even laugh very loud, unless I'm caught off guard, and I'm rarely caught off guard.

Maybe it's because my siblings were given to overly dramatic responses, and I never felt like there was enough room in our home to add my own feelings to the mix; so, I learned how to keep mine zipped in and buttoned up. But the more you stuff things inside the more likely it is that all those things will bust out and make a really big mess one day.

Welcome to my mid-life crisis. Did I forget to mention I turned forty that year?

Well I did, the last day of November. A couple months later a good friend of mine died without warning. Her name was Lexi, and she was only thirty-four. February was kind of a blur for those of us who knew and loved Lexi, and Tanner, and the four kids he was now raising all by himself. I remember how terrifying it was to be alone those first couple of weeks. So much for writing. I was no longer able to stay home and concentrate while my kids were in school and my husband was at work. Instead I went to lots of yoga classes and hung out at the church office and cried with my friends. We all seemed to need each other's presence more than usual.

In March I distracted myself from all the sadness in my heart by trying to get a book contract. My friend Rebecca introduced me to her agent, so I sent him some of my work and we exchanged a few phone calls. He told me that he loved my writing, but since I didn't have a very big platform, perhaps I needed a bigger idea. "Christian publishers aren't very interested in memoir," he told me. "They'd rather make books that have a definable take away," he said, "because those books are more likely to sell in the Christian market." As I reread my stories and tried to brainstorm, I noticed a theme running through many of the essays I'd written in the past ten years–the importance of lament.

In April, I got really sick with an upper respiratory virus. It was terrible; I stayed in bed for most of the month. On weekends I rallied enough for church and small group meetings, but come Monday I was passed out in front of the TV again. When I could think clearly, I tried to come up with that all important 'take-away' the agent had described. I had a couple of ideas, but I never called to discuss them. I didn't know if I had enough to say about grief or lamentation to write a whole book. Besides, it's not like I was an expert, or had done extensive research on those topics. I just knew some of the lessons I'd learned through exploring them.

Like how the more you try to ignore grief, the stronger it becomes. Grief was, in my experience, the most tangible emotion–an actual presence I felt, much more than love, joy, sadness, or pain. I've heard many people describe grief as a fog, the way it tends to blur your vision and cloud your mind. You can't seem to see or think clearly anymore when you're in the throes of grief. You can literally feel its heaviness in your heart, its lump in your throat, its churning in your stomach. When you're in the midst of a grieving season your days have an extra layer of thickness as you move through them, and your sleepless nights begin to feel darker–in ways you can't adequately describe.

When the first waves of grief for Sam hit me, I felt like a wooly little lamb, all alone, in the middle of the Mississippi river. The cold black water was up to my neck and I was gasping for air, flailing my hooves around, searching for something to hold onto that would keep me afloat. I woke up and ate the book of Psalms for breakfast. I couldn't swallow regular food until I'd seen the words of David. I understood the sadness of his repetition in a new way. I knew what it meant to long for some sort of divine rescue, *more than watchmen wait for the morning, more than watchmen wait for the morning.* My time with God felt less like worship and more like resuscitation, and it hurt to have his holy breath blown into my lungs, but I didn't know what else to do. If God couldn't be real to me in those moments, he would never be real to me again.

There was so much to do when May rolled around that I didn't have any time left for sadness. The end of the school year is usually crazy for our family; and for me, graduation became just another item to check off the list. I'd anticipated the sadness of it so much that when it actually came all I could feel was proud, and that was a blessing. For several weeks I'd seen my friends celebrating with their seniors on social media, and each picture felt like another punch in the gut. From the first spring formal to the last baccalaureate ceremony, I'd felt left out. Finally, graduation was something we got to participate in, too.

In June Sam changed her name on Facebook and announced to the world that she was transgender. Sam had shared these wishes with me and John eighteen months before that, but we'd been hoping and praying that she would change her mind. A couple of weeks after that we went to the beach for a family vacation, and I took along a book to read as a distraction, not realizing how appropriate it would be for this particular transition.

The book was about a man whose father died during the middle of a legal separation from his wife, brought on by her infidelity. The man's family was Jewish, and his mother told him that his father's dying wish was for the whole family to "sit Shiva" in honor of his passing. Many of the rituals of Shiva date back to Bible days, like having immediate family members of the recently deceased sit in chairs with shorter legs than the chairs of the well-wishers who come to visit–in order to symbolize how low their grief had brought them. The priest also covered all the mirrors in the house so mourners would not be distracted by things of lesser importance, like vanity.

My favorite of the rituals mentioned in the book was the Shiva candle. The priest came and lit it every morning during the week of mourning, except for Sabbath, when the family was allowed a break from grieving, and got to go to the temple with their friends and extended families. The candle struck me as a meaningful symbol of grief. When the priest first showed up with it everyone was surprised at how big the candle was, and I thought about how you can't predict the exact amount of time it takes for a candle to burn. It all depends on how long and how often you light it, how well you trim the wick, and how much wind the flame is exposed to. Also, the thought of grief as a flame makes perfect sense, because of its equal potential for damage or good.

No one looks forward to grief. We don't get excited about leaning into our pain, but when sorrow is continually denied, it has the potential to set a whole life on fire. Unacknowledged hurt can be a breeding ground for all sorts of unhealthy habits, some you don't even realize you've picked up. Like the way the right side of my jaw started aching, from being clenched most of the time.

Sam turned eighteen in July, and I got tired of trying to navigate this grief river all by myself, so I decided to go see a therapist again. I'd already been meeting with a mentor every few weeks for most of the year and having long talks over coffee with a couple of other mothers of seniors, and praying with some friends in my small group, but all those things weren't enough anymore. What I needed now was a guide to lead me through the process of lament.

As this book attests, I've gone through this process a number of times over the years, with various kinds of counselors. Not every situation was the best fit, but I've never regretted the opportunity to be heard and understood. As demonstrated through many of my stories, I'm not very good at sharing my heart or my true feelings with anyone, not even myself. So sometimes it takes the help of a guide to pull out all the emotions I keep hidden inside. I used to blame the culture I grew up in, but now I know better. God's been trying to teach people the importance of lament since the days of Job, but we still don't get it.

We moved Sam into her dorm room at UTC on August 17th. It was my husband's fortieth birthday, and one of the hardest days we've shared during our twenty years together. Also, I freaked out a little bit. As in, throw the dog gate down the stairs, yell at your clueless pets, and sob into your sweater for half an hour once you get inside the minivan, kind of freak out. Thankfully Sam was driving her own car to Chattanooga; because I was not prepared for a nice goodbye just yet. Even though I'd written in my journal most days, gone to yoga twice a week, and practiced surrender over and over for the previous year, I still didn't know how to say goodbye to the first baby I ever loved, the first toddler who called me Mommy, the first kid who thought I actually hung the moon. There's no adequate preparation you can do for a day like that. It's going to hurt like hell, even under the best circumstances.

Which is exactly what I said to my mentor when she texted me to see how I was doing the day before. "It hurts like hell," I typed, because I couldn't pull my punches anymore. If she really wanted to know, I had to really tell her. Yet her response to me was full of grace and truth. "I know," she said. "It's a really rough one."

Sitting with someone in grief feels too passive to be meaningful, but it's truly the best gift you can give them. In a world that's constantly calling us to move on to the next fun thing, the next shiny adventure—because the best time of your life is just around the corner—it takes a steely resolve to give someone more than an hour or two of your time. But being present with a friend during his sorrow is like giving him a ring of gold, or a piece of silver.

The last chapter of Job tells us that the friends and family who came to visit him after God restored his fortune brought him rings of gold and pieces of silver. It's such a strange thing to imagine because it must have been years after the tragedy—it's not like Job needed any more treasures—but his loved ones were still trying to comfort him. In verse eleven it says that they did so because of "all the adversity that the Lord had brought upon him." Let that sink in for a minute, God did this to Job. Yes, the devil started it, but God said he could. The God of Abraham, Isaac, and Jacob is also the God of Job and he's a God who allows his children to feel pain, and loss, and hurt, and grief, and sorrow. Sometimes he's even responsible for it, but he's also the one who promises to be with us during those dark times.

Like when the doctor says there's nothing more he can do, or when a husband confesses to an affair. When a teenager ends his own life, or a brother is arrested for drunk driving. When parents file for divorce, when pregnancies end without a healthy baby. When you've lost your job again, when you miss the family you had to leave behind, when you can't seem to find anyone to start a family with in the first place. When family members are abusive and selfish and mean, and you don't know how to love them anymore, when forgiveness and healing seem impossible. These are the troubles of this world, the rivers of grief we must cross, and no amount of theology, good or bad, keeps us dry when we're in the middle of them. Even though Jesus overcame this world, and all the dark times in it, this broken world still makes us sad.

And it's okay to be sad. Like the prophet Jeremiah said, you can't bandage a wound superficially and act like everything is fine when everything is not fine. But what does it look like to "take heart," like Jesus told his disciples to do in the gospel of John? To be filled with hope while still acknowledging the depth of your troubles?

I guess it can look like lots of different things, and maybe one of those is buying a puppy, but maybe another is being honest with your friends—trusting them to help you carry your grief burden from time to time. And maybe another is making the choice to look for God in the middle of your Mississippi river, even when you feel like he's not there at all. Psalms tells us that God collects our tears in a bottle, that we can pour out our hearts to him, that he's with us in the darkness—and—it does not feel dark to him. So, I believe it's an act of worship, a declaration of hope any time you lift your eyes up... to the hills... to the maker of heaven and earth—even if you don't say anything particularly worshipful. In fact, you don't have to say anything at all. Some sorrows only come out in tears and moans, in breaking things, and giving up, yet Jesus understands it all. His own Spirit translates for us, and he knows exactly which lambs need to be carried for a while, until we reach the other shore.

Postscript

I was attending a writing conference in April of 2018, when I finally began to understand the theme for this book I'd been trying to write for eight years. The conference was in Michigan, a ten-hour drive north for me, and much colder than the Spring I'd left behind in Knoxville. As I trudged across the campus of Calvin College, through wet globs of snow and blustering bitter winds, I thought about how hard it was to keep going sometimes, when the weather of life threatens to knock you down.

On the drive home it rained for several hours straight, but the sun shone briefly just after I stopped for lunch, so I switched CDs and turned up the music. The poetry of Mark Heard captured my heart as I drove the windy highway home. I'm not sure what all of his songs are about, but anyone who can sing the word "jacaranda" and make it rhyme with something, is worth listening to in my book.

Before long the music began to make me cry. I missed my husband, and couldn't wait to tell him about my weekend at the conference. I wished he'd been able to go with me. I remembered the faces of the beautiful women who'd shared their poetry with me and thought about how much I love words. I was tired of driving, and ready to pull over for a nap when I heard the refrain from "Strong Hand of Love."

The words made me think of Sam, whom I hadn't seen since Christmas. I longed for Sam to hear these words and be struck by their truth. How life is hard and wonderful, and we can't always find it in our hearts to believe there's a great goodness behind it all, but that's okay. It doesn't mean that goodness isn't still here, hidden in the shadows.

And then I wanted to write a letter to the whole world saying the same thing. A letter filled with my own struggles to learn this truth: that just because the book of life is filled with thorns, that doesn't mean its author is a heartless monster. Which, if I'm being honest, is how I felt for many years about God. So much of the advice I heard from other Christians shrugged off the pain and hurt of this world. They kept telling me to ignore the blood dripping from my fingers because the roses in my hand were so beautiful. And yes, the roses of the gospel are beautiful, but when your eyes are filled with tears, that truth can be hard to see.

Because there's a difference between genuinely denying the sinful tendencies of your flesh, and simply pretending they don't exist. Because we humans are more than mere souls dressed in three-dimensional skin costumes. And these bodies we inhabit are arguably the most intentional element of our earthly experience. You can spend your life ignoring that body, but eventually, it finds a way to get your attention. For me that happened when I found myself in the middle of a dark depression six months after Sam was born.

It forced me to seek out the help of a therapist who actually became Jesus to me, rather than just another teacher who told me all about him. And it was her flesh and blood, her time and attention, her listening ears and her peaceful voice who saved me from myself and helped me find hope and faith once more. A solid faith, with space to grow and breathe, and keep me standing upright, until I fly away to the real heaven someday, the place where grief and lament are no longer necessary.

Jeremiah 6: 14 talks about the pious priests of Israel, how they dealt falsely with themselves and each other, treating harsh wounds as though they were not serious: "'Peace, peace,' they say, when there is no peace."

I'm afraid that's how many people of faith feel about their emotional wounds today as well. They're looking for permission to acknowledge the hardness of life, so they can find hope for the future.

When I finally got permission to take care of those thorny cuts in my own life, I was able to get to a place where I could focus on the beauty of the roses again. It's a place where joy and sadness are both allowed inside my heart, and I don't have to be afraid of them anymore. For the only way to get from pain to hope is to walk through grief. That's what good grief is, the kind that helps you move out of a place of mourning, and back into a place of real life.

And real life is good, even though it's painful. Which is an easy sentence to write, but a hard one to believe. After all, I don't know what your life is like. I don't know what kind of pain you've been through, and I can't force anyone to believe anything I say. I can only tell you about the journey I've been on the past several years. And maybe it won't turn out to be true for you. I'm not making any guarantees here. I don't have a seven-step formula or a five-minute take away. I only have my stories. I only have the truth that Love has shown me, and if you saw me sitting here in the coffee shop today you might see a little tear in the corner of my eye. Because I'm not whole yet. I'm still a work in progress. 'Til the day I no longer have to ask the question, "Why?" On that day I'll finally get to sleep underneath another sky. It's one I've never seen before, and I don't know if it will be anything like the "satellite sky" Mark Heard sings about, but I've heard there's an endless amount of light.

Acknowledgments

Writing this book was an eight-year journey, so there are a lot of people to thank for helping me finally get it out into the world.

First and foremost is my best friend and husband, John. He's my first reader and my best critic. John's been cheering me on for twenty-four years! Thank you, honey, for all the motivational talks and putting up with my pity parties. You're my one true companion, and I'll love you forever.

I'm also grateful to Adam Whipple, Lorraine Furtner, Jill Kovalchick, Matthew and April Cyr, Jeanine Joyner, and the rest of the Knox Writes/ Foundling House Crew. You've all made me a better writer and friend.

Thanks to my publisher, John Palmer Gregg, and his wife Tina, for editorial help, keen insight, and ongoing support in bringing this book to life. Thank you also for being kindred spirits, and for reading, caring, and listening. Here's to many more fun projects together!

A very special thanks to Susan Tucker and Lori Douthat. Susan, you've been my best writing friend and encourager for over ten years. Thank you for believing in me and helping me make all those corrections! Lori, you've heard more about this book than most, yet you always show interest and enthusiasm. I appreciate your point of view and all the ways you take care of me. Thanks also for all the photos!

Writing a book about the story of your life is a vulnerable process, and I'm indebted to so many members and artists from the Rabbit Room community for showing me example after example of how to tell the truth and tell it well. There are too many of you to list everyone, but I'd like to mention some by name, like: Andrew Peterson, Pete Peterson, Matt Conner, Carrie Givens, Rebecca Reynolds, Kris Camealy, Jonathan Rogers, Eric Peters, Jennifer Trafton, Helena Sorenson, Jill Phillips, Thomas McKenzie, Russ Ramsey, Hope Kemp, Sally Zaengle, Dawn Green, AE Graham, Kate Hinson, Kim Fisher, John Cal, Laura Preston, Laura Peterson, Dave and Leanne Bruno, Ashley Barber, and Tricia Prinzi.

Finally, to all those who played a part in helping me cross the finish line, like my Beta Readers: Janet Gregg, Angie Baker, Bethani Lufi, Judy Parker, Debbie Moody, Kevin Still, Faith Tyler, Ginger Hare, Haley Moore, Jen Yokel, Leah Phillipi, Dawn Morrow, Suzanne Tietjen, Ellen Bright, Leigh Anne Burley, Sarah Gardener, Lynn Holloway, Katherine Kamin, and Jerusalem Greer; my launch team members, especially Mary Beth Eiler for leading the campaign; and other friends who've shared their talents with me, like Laney Barber, Hayden Zelem, Michelle De Rusha, Laura Brown, and Katie Brunone.

To all the pastors, therapists, and friends who show up in these pages. Thank you for letting me use your real names and for being the very real people that you are to me.

And finally, to Mom and Dad. You two have taken the biggest risk to support this book, and it means the world that you chose to stand by me. May I give that same gift to my own kids someday.

One last word for Sam, Laney, and Ben: You three are the best and most undeniable blessings I've ever known. May the same Jesus who made me your Mom reach into your hearts and heal the places where my human love falls short.

Lightning Source UK Ltd.
Milton Keynes UK
UKHW022206021220
374515UK00011BA/2459